D1491550

The Great Escape

The Ten Secrets to Loving your Life and Living your Dreams

GEOFF THOMPSON

SUMMERSDALE

Summersdale Publishers Ltd
46 West Street
Chichester
West Sussex
PO19 1RP
UK

www.summersdale.com

www.geoffthompson.com

Printed and bound in Great Britain.

ISBN 1 84024 180 2

Cartoons by John Smyth

About the Author

Geoff Thompson has written over 20 published books and is known worldwide for his bestselling autobiography *Watch My Back*, about his nine years working as a nightclub doorman. He currently has a quarter of a million books in print. He holds the rank of 6th Dan black belt in Japanese karate, 1st Dan in judo and is also qualified to senior instructor level in various other forms of wrestling and martial arts. He has several scripts for stage, screen and TV in development with Destiny Films.

He has published several articles for *GQ* magazine, and has also been featured in *FHM*, *Maxim*, *Arena*, *Front* and *Loaded* magazines, and has appeared many times on mainstream television.

Geoff is currently a contributing editor for *Men's Fitness* magazine.

Other books and videos
by Geoff Thompson

Books:

Watch My Back *The Geoff Thompson Autobiography*
The Elephant and the Twig – *The Art of Positive Thinking. 14 Golden Rules to Success and Happiness*
A Book for the Seriously Stressed – *How to Stop Stress from Killing You* (Previously published as **Small Wars**)
Fear – The Friend of Exceptional People *Techniques in Controlling Fear*
The Formula – Spiritual Guidance
Real Grappling
Real Punching
Real Kicking
Real Head, Knees & Elbows
Dead or Alive – Self-protection
Three Second Fighter – The Sniper Option
Weight Training – For the Martial Artist
The Pavement Arena
Animal Day – Pressure Testing the Martial Arts
Blue Blood on the Mat by Athol Oakley, Foreword by Geoff Thompson
The Fence
The Art of Fighting Without Fighting
The Throws and Takedowns of Judo
The Throws and Takedowns of Sambo-Russian Wrestling
The Throws and Takedowns of Freestyle Wrestling
The Throws and Takedowns of Greco-Roman Wrestling
The Ground Fighting Series
Pins: The Bedrock
The Escapes
Chokes and Strangles
Arm Bars and Joint Locks
Fighting From Your Back
Fighting From Your Knees

Videos:

Animal Day – Pressure Testing the Martial Arts
Animal Day Part Two – The Fights
Three Second Fighter – The Sniper Option
Throws and Takedowns Vols. 1- 6
Real Punching Vols. 1-3
The Fence

Ground Fighting Series
Vol 1 Pins: The Bedrock
Vol 2 The Escapes
Vol 3 Chokes and Strangles
Vol 4 Arm Bars and Joint Locks
Vol 5 Fighting From Your Back
Vol 6 Fighting From Your Knees

Advanced Ground Fighting Vols. 1-3
Pavement Arena Part 1
Pavement Arena Part 2 – The Protection Pyramid
Pavement Arena Part 3 – Grappling. The Last Resort
Pavement Arena Part 4 – Fit To Fight

For more details visit www.geoffthompson.com

For a free colour brochure of Geoff Thompson products ring/fax 02476 431100 or write
to Geoff Thompson @ PO Box 307 Coventry, West Midlands CV3 2YP.

Acknowledgements

I'd like to start by thanking Hannah Lewis for doing such a fantastic and impartial job in editing this book. If it weren't for Hannah your head would be spinning with mixed metaphors and base-less proverbs probably within minutes (possibly even milliseconds) of opening this book.

I'd like to also say thank you to Stacey Wood for doing a meticulous job of typing this book from four badly spelt reporter pads of handwritten text.

Thank you to all the staff on the *Sunbird* cruise liner (Air Tours), especially Captain Philip Rentell for making our stay such a fantastic one. Also thanks to Sujeet for looking after us in Lido's restaurant onboard ship.

Hi to Lynn and Gemma Christie, two lovely friends from the *Sunbird*.

Thanks to Ged and Norma for their lovely company over breakfast and by the pool.

Thank you to my gorgeous daughter Kerry Thompson for doing such a great first edit on this book.

Thanks also to my beautiful son Louis for coming up with the name 'The Great Escape'. Thanks mate.

Thanks to my all my lovely friends at Summersdale for their constant support. Especially Stewart and Alastair for first publishing my work and guiding me.

Thank you most of all to God. I love you God.

Dedication

To my beautiful angel Sharon. I love you so much.

To my lovely friend Michael from Huddersfield, I hope this book helps you to make your great escape.

– Contents –

– Preface –

4 a.m. Barbados – 2 January 2001

Welcome to *The Great Escape*. I thought it might be appropriate to start (and in fact write) my new book about loving your life and living your dreams from the upper deck of the sea cruising ship the *Sunbird* (actually it is less of a ship and more of a small city). At present it is cutting through the Caribbean Sea on its way to Aruba – somewhere hot and exotic off Venezuela.

When I told Sharon that I was writing *The Great Escape* from the deck of the *Sunbird* she warned me to be careful on two counts. I always listen to her; she has a womanly knack of being bull's-eye right. On the first point she warned, 'Be careful you don't fall overboard.' Me? She based warning number one on the fact that I can't put on my boxers in the morning without catching my big toe in the waistband and taking half of the bedroom furniture with me when I fall. I heeded her warning. At 4 a.m., in the dark, with only the stars to guide our way (OK, there are lights on the ship – artistic licence and all that) swimming home to Coventry would test even my reserve, not to mention my front crawl.

Her second point though, whilst logged and noted, I had to disagree with. 'Geoff,' she said, 'it's pissing down with rain at home in England and brass monkeys are investing in blowtorches. You'll upset people no end if you even make mention of a Caribbean cruise – let alone the fact that we are on one!' I rarely disagree with Sharon (she's a 4th Dan black belt, it wouldn't be healthy) but on this occasion I had to. I made the point that the Caribbean is exactly the place I should write my book from. The premise of *The Great Escape* is that we should all be loving our life and living our dreams, and as I sit here sipping hot coffee – not too sweet please – with the warm West Indies trade winds blowing across my brow, I realise that I am doing exactly that. Me, the kid from the factory, the man from the nightclub door, the bloke who wrote 'that' book – *Watch My Back*. If I can do it anyone can. Anyone!

There are just a few elements that need to be in place.

In this book, I would like to explore these secret elements to attaining success in whatever form you would like it.

The information herein is not hypothesis, it is not a sickly-sweet philosophy that will melt under the heat of reality; all the information typed meticulously into these pages is experience-based knowledge. It's how I live my life. It is my hope that, in reading this text, you will be better able to love *your* life and live *your* dreams also.

– Introduction –

The elephant is trained from an early age, when its brain is still pliable enough to be influenced, in the art of limitation. Its trainers realise that if they are to control a beast that weighs more than a large car – dozens of times the size and weight of themselves – then they have to catch it very young. They have to make it believe that, despite its bulk and irrespective of its immense power, it is helplessly weak when tethered, even to a twig.

They achieve their aim by roping the young elephant to huge immovable objects, like very large trees, so that it is held back every time it tries to escape or to explore. The elephant tries so hard and so often – only to fail time and again – that eventually it believes itself incapable of escape. It develops what is known as 'learned helplessness'. As a fully matured adult, weighing more than two politicians after a party conference buffet (pretty heavy!), it can be tied to a twig and it won't escape, in fact it won't even try.

As I explained in *The Elephant and the Twig*, we are often the same, and while our training in the art of limitation is often inadvertent or subconscious, it is no less restricting. As fledglings, our influences (people and environment) become our trainers and mostly they teach us what they know (which is not always much) and what they believe (which is not always true). Hence we tend to become a product of our environment, a mirror image of those who wean us.

As a species we have a great and natural knack of adapting to and even mimicking our surroundings, though this is not necessarily always healthy. If you don't believe me go into a supermarket on any busy Friday when trolleys are bashing trolleys, children are crying and mothers are fretting in long checkout lines, and tell me that you don't quickly make like the locals, pick up the pace and go into stressed-and-snappy mode yourself. Paradoxically, we drove through Barbados yesterday on the way to our cruise ship and the opposite occurred. Very quickly a bus full of hot and bothered tourists looking for an injection of calm after an eight-hour flight and an eighteen-hour (total) journey, quickly became natives and chilled. The guy driving the coach was the coolest man I ever met. He beeped hello to other vehicles we passed, even stopped the bus on several occasions just to speak with friends on the side of the road; he seemed to know everyone. I have never seen so many people relax so quickly and so completely. And why? Because the immediate influences were strong, and they felt compelled to fall into line, which in this case (unlike the Friday night shopping story) is fantastic.

Take the same bus of people to a place where high-stress and fast-pace come with the coffee and the chilled tourists would very quickly heat up to the temperature of their influencing surroundings and probably be swapping leather within minutes.

We adapt to our environment, it's how we survive, and it is how we are taught. But it doesn't have to be this way. You can unlearn the bad habits of upbringing, you can shed that old and weathered skin and you can re-educate yourself into a powerful, creative and very happy individual with the muscle to shape worlds (and uproot twigs).

Sometimes, when elephants get fed up of being controlled by trainers and when they tire of being tied to twigs (like the fellow on the front of this book), they decide to do something about it. They probably wake up one day and realise, 'Hey, I weigh several tons. I'm massive! I don't have to take this shit.' And so they start by releasing themselves from their twig by giving it a determined pull, thus setting their souls free to contemplate the great and wonderful unknown (like the fellow on the back of this book).

We are products of our upbringing. If our early training was in the art of limitation then, as adults, we often feel disempowered. And of course if we *feel* disempowered we are, because it is our thoughts that dictate our world. What we have to realise is that, like the elephant who escaped, we are no longer captives; no one has the authority to control us any more. We have the awesome power not only to break that metaphoric but very limiting twig, we also have the muscle to snatch it clean out of the ground, mud, roots and all and to make our escape. The Great Escape.

As a species we have the ability to change the world, certainly our own world, and of this I have no doubt. In fact I am a living embodiment of my live-it-now do-it-all philosophy. I live my life in the creation business (I create my world) and I love every minute of it. Thus far I have managed to make manifest every desire I have set my intention on. This is not meant to sound smug. I see myself as a very ordinary person who has managed to liberate himself from a life of unnecessary toil. If I can do it, believe me, anyone can.

I measure my accomplishment not by the balance in my bank (though lots of noughts can be very pleasing), rather I measure my lot by the fact that when I get up in the morning and when I go to bed last thing at night I feel happy. That's what makes me a success.

As a child I always dreamed of making my living as a writer, a wordsmith, a crafter of letters; as an adult that is exactly what places bread on my table from one day to the next. Success, of course, is very subjective. Your idea of nirvana may be – and very probably is – entirely different from mine. As long as what you do makes you happy and doesn't harm others then it would be fair to say you are a success. It's only when you spend your life doing the things you don't like to do that the Monday-morning-feeling stretches through until Friday afternoon and then Sundays are a horror because they precede Monday (if you see what I mean). That's when you find yourself thinking: is this what I really want to do with my life? Especially if you feel your nine-to-five is a must-do, and that you are only there because you feel you have no other choice.

People are forever telling me that they would love to write, to sculpt, to garden, to teach but they can't because their life, their wife, the mortgage, the kids, their environment, circumstances or even God won't allow it. The very statement 'I can't' is one I used to death as a younger man and by its very nature it becomes a self-fulfilling prophecy. It is probably the most overused and certainly the most disempowering combination of words you could ever make the mistake of employing because it does exactly what it says on the tin. If you can't because your wife says so then you give her all your power, meaning that until she says 'yes' you're stuck where you are. If you blame the environment, circumstance or your upbringing you give all your power over to these intangibles because, again, it means that until they favour you, you're glued to mediocrity. If you believe you are powerless then by definition you are exactly that.

The reason I know this is because I have fallen into the same trap more times than I care to remember. As a youngster I spent my days wallowing in procrastination, blame and self-pity – I hated my lot but, of course, my lot was never my fault (is it ever?).

So my motivation for writing this book is that I learned my lesson early on and made good. I feel suitably qualified therefore, to suggest that it doesn't have to be this way, you don't have to spend the rest of your life at the proverbial grindstone.

The answer is as simple as ABC; take back the responsibility for your own creative power. Admit ownership of your future then set about building a palatial existence that makes you happy, and by extension makes all those you love happy also. It takes bollocks of cast iron to take the reins, but if you want to trail-blaze then being in the saddle is where it's at.

Think about the job you do for one moment. You probably spend two-thirds (at least) of your waking life in work. Two-thirds! Now if you don't love the bones off your job, if you are not inspired to the point of exhilaration about the nuts and bolts of your employ, if they don't have to drag you away from the office kicking and screaming at the end of each day because you want to do more, then you have to ask yourself: Why am I here? And just hope that your first answer is not, 'The money!' I am emphatic about this message so please don't think me conceited when I tell you that I love my lot. I love being me – but it wasn't always this way. I spent the first half of my life living other people's idea of normal and I hated it to pieces. Now I enjoy myself so much I don't want to go to bed at night, I want to be out there experiencing everything. You see, when you love what you do it stops being work, it's fun. It's unconventional certainly; unpredictable definitely; sometimes it scares the living poo out of me for sure. But I like unconventional, I thrive on the unpredictability and, if I am being honest here, I like being scared (admittedly the poo bit can get messy). I love being overwhelmed, even out of my depth. I have become comfortable with discomfort because it's a sign that I am growing. I don't want to be stuck in the middle of some cornflake-sized comfort-zone sweeping around an oily, cranking machine and praying for tea break – I want to be precariously balanced on some craggy precipice where I can see it all.

'Yeah I agree,' you may concede (followed closely by the obligatory BUT), 'but it's really hard.'

Of course it's hard, it has to be hard. You can't temper a blade without putting it through a forge. What's the use of a ribbon when you haven't run the race? It is hard, but please, let's keep things in perspective here: carrying a hod on a building site is back-breakingly hard, working your brain into mush on a computer every day can be hard with a capital H. In fact any job – especially if you despise it – that entails bargaining two-thirds of your incarnation just to pay the mortgage is harder than a big bag of hard things. We all know about hard. It's what we do on a daily basis. At least when your sweat is vocational, when you are hacking away in the right jungle, then you can sit down at the end of another satisfying day and think, 'This is what I really want to do with my life.'

We are where we are in life through choice (even if it is just the fact that we do not choose to change where we are, or at least change our perception of it). If we don't like it we have the God-given power to reinvent ourselves – the moment we think that we lack this power our thoughts make it so. Some dead famous person (so famous I can't even remember his name) once said, 'If you think you can or you think you can't you are right.'

So go ahead; think that you can, and you might be pleasantly surprised to find that you are right.

The Power of Intention

6.30 a.m. St Lucia – 3 January 2001

Whilst most people are still asleep in bed, St Lucia – or more specifically the island's inhabitants – are water-skiing and yachting into a new day.

How many times have you heard people say, 'I'd love to do that. What a life.' They say it with a sense that it will never happen, that it could never be.

In reality, St Lucia is no more than a day away by plane from just about anywhere in this world. If your intention is to wake up to green mountains and turquoise seas then you are as good as there. If your desire becomes your intention then St Lucia better watch out. It's not about money. Money is not the problem: lack of belief and faith are. Belief and faith in your ability to love your life and live your dreams will smash down the barriers – imposed or supposed – that stand in your path. In fact, if your intention is strong enough, the barriers will melt before your very eyes. Our dreams are only an intention away.

I had a chap write to me about travelling to America to realise his dream of training with the famous Machado brothers (a legendary martial arts family). A dream courted, though not often realised, by many aspiring martial artists. His story was a familiar one of desire laced with the disappointment in his belief that only a lottery win or an unexpected windfall would make his dreams become reality. He held the same beliefs as many: the mortgage, the car payments and his parents were immovable objects tying him to a life that he didn't want to lead. If it wasn't for them (he believed) he'd be gone in a heartbeat.

If he didn't have these excuses there would most certainly have been a host of other excuses why he couldn't go. It is not the hurdles and pitfalls that block our path to our goal, it's the fact that we fail to overcome them that keeps us where we are. Then he read *The Elephant and the Twig*.

The letter that popped through my letterbox tingled in my fingers. The energy almost fired the words off the paper. It was from my erstwhile friend and the card was from America where he was training with the Machados. He was so excited, he couldn't believe he was there. But he was and he had got there by moving every obstacle until the path was clear. The strength he gained from the journey was what brought the destination into being.

It is by overcoming these obstacles that we develop the physique to handle and cope with our success. A man that wants to lift a 200lb bar-bell must be prepared to develop the musculature to handle that weight. He must develop a 200lb mentality. To take this kind of weight off the rack without the right mentality and physique is to court injury and disappointment. If you have obstacles in your path they are there for a reason. It is not in acquiring a million pounds that you become a millionaire, rather it is in overcoming the obstacles in your way.

People often talk of desire, of want, even of need, but very few talk about intention. As a younger man I was no different. I wanted more, I desired it, at times I even needed it, but I never really intended to get it. Like the masses, I sat behind the twitching curtains of suburbia and waited for providence to knock on my door. Then, like the many, I moaned and complained when my wants never materialised.

Why was life so unkind to me? Why were the five per cent wearing bespoke suits and living their dreams, whilst I lived a hand-me-down existence in the lower echelons? It took me a long time to realise there existed and eventually to traverse the cavernous gulf between desire and intention. Like many (and like the elephant) I felt powerless. I felt like someone had cut my Samsonian locks and I was trapped by the belief that my destiny was both rooted and immovable.

Then I learned about the frightening 'power of intention', and the fact that if I fully intended – with every cell in my body – to do something, then mountains would move and seas would part.

Desire is such an empty and impotent emotion. It wants, but is not prepared to do anything to manifest its wants, preferring instead to sit and wait for the Lottery finger to point in its direction. And sometimes it does, but then at the last second the finger of fortune goes palm up and gives us the 'up yours' sign. Desire, when it's not attached to a solid intention, does the opposite to what it says on the tin. Rather than attract our dreams, it creates a centrifugal force that pushes them away. Why does it do this? Probably because we haven't built the cerebral physique to carry the weight of our desire. Life protects us in our ignorance; it doesn't send us parcels that we are not strong enough to open. If you want to be a millionaire you have to develop a millionaire mentality.

In my youth I remember telling my wife that when I 'made it' I was going to make like Houdini and disappear, go somewhere where the phone didn't ring and people were scarce. I was so tired of the daily slog that I wanted to buy myself out of it with a providential fortune. I fell into the old trap of saying, 'If I had a million pounds I'd never work again.' Which was precisely why I never made a million quid. The Universe has a great knack of not giving us any more than we can handle. The Universe rarely places more discs on the bar-bell than we can lift. Simply by saying, 'With a bit of cash I'd stop work,' we are not only saying, 'I couldn't handle the million,' we are also saying, 'Actually, I'm struggling with the weight I've already got.' It is the paradox of intent and surrender. We fully intend something to happen but we surrender the final outcome to a greater force than ourselves. Like a farmer planting seeds, he intends them to grow, but ultimately he is governed by something bigger and he surrenders to that force secure in the knowledge that all outcomes will be for a reason. It seems like a contradiction, but this is how it all works. If I fully intend something to happen, and it doesn't, I trust that it is because there is something even better for me around the corner.

Think of your dreams as a Christmas list (I'll talk about lists later). You are very unlikely to get anything that is not written down; if you haven't written it down then you haven't asked for it. And it needs to be very clearly written. The dreams that have little doubts circling all around them say to anyone with half an intellect, 'I think I want this but I'm not entirely sure.' Can you handle the weight of your dreams? Be very clear before you write them down (or ask for them). In fact write down the consequences of having what you want at the same time so that you are aware of the cost. If the majority of us were suddenly granted three wishes (and we were unaware of the added consequence of realising them) our problems would likely triple.

A farmer that has one field of corn may dream of owning ten fields – and he can surely have them if his intent is clear – but could he handle ten if providence popped them in his Christmas sack? Preparing the land for planting seed in one field is entirely different to preparing the land for ten times one. The work will be tenfold and unless the farmer does a little delegation the planting would take much longer. There would be ten times more work and even when it came time to reap the harvest, one man could find a lot of problems reaping ten fields.

This is not meant to put you off. Please don't feel I am being negative. Mine is an empirical and objective, certainly a pragmatic look at the responsibility of success (or having ten fields to plough when you are under-equipped, physically and otherwise). Like the cruise liner I am sat on at this very second (cutting through the Caribbean ocean, so smoothly you hardly know you are at sea). It carries – at any one time – several thousand passengers of all ages (lots of very young people like me), sex (yes please), and denomination. It is a huge ship with six restaurants, two swimming pools, badminton courts, basketball on deck, shops, casinos, blah-de-blah. You get the picture. It is a big baby. Ships like this don't just simply appear out of thin air. You couldn't run the local ferry (six passengers, one driver, no refreshments) and 'wish' to own a cruise liner without any thought of the consequence, because as a ferryboat owner you are not equipped, with staff or otherwise, to handle that kind of success. Not at the moment anyway. So when the ferry owner places 'sea-faring-cruise-liner please' on his list of wishes he is not thinking it through. He is not looking at the consequences of having his dream.

My friend once said to me, 'I'd love a V8 Jag!' I think a lot of people would, it is a great dream, and actually managing to buy a new one is not beyond comprehension. Let's say that now, this moment, providence plonked a racing green (beige leather interior) XK8 on you drive and said, 'Did you order this?' Would you, could you, cope with it? Could you make the servicing costs (thousands of pounds), the maintenance (more thousands), even the cost of putting petrol in the tank could break the bank if it doesn't contain a healthy wad. Again, not negative, not pessimistic, just realistic. I believe that anyone can have a Jag (or whatever car they want) if they intend to have it. But when you do, things change. Even the people around you will treat you differently when you own a nice new car. Jealousy, envy and cynicism are a familiar trinity when you reach from the mud to the stars.

Can you handle owning a car emotionally? Sounds stupid, I know. People always laugh when I ask this. The usual response is a sardonic grin, followed by, 'Geoff, I think I can handle a top of the range, luxury vehicle, thank you very much!' They think I am being patronising when I ask the question. But could you handle the fact that your dream has suddenly, with no work (at this point I am still talking about a providential gift), been made manifest?

Let me try and explain. All of the early lunar astronauts had emotional problems after their flights into space because their life ambition of going to the moon was suddenly realised. When they came back down to earth – literally and metaphorically – many of them became depressed and bewildered. I mean, where do you go from there?

When you get the Jag (or whatever) it is a similar life goal. To many people, the goal of owning a £50,000 car is as big as going to the moon. Once you've got it, what's left for you to do next? Then there's the guilt of owning the kind of vehicle that royalty and pop stars drive. When I got my first Land Rover Discovery, a luxury car by anyone's standards, I felt bad for weeks. I actually felt guilty. I felt as though I didn't deserve such a beautiful car, owning it was too big for my mentality. I got used to it (I've had four now), but at the time I felt very low. Owning the car also affected the people around me. Some of my friends were unhappy about my sudden climb from the torn front seat of a rusting Ford Sierra to the leather, heated seats of a dream machine that cost more than their homes. I remember the week I got it. I went to breakfast with one of my old friends; I couldn't wait to share my good fortune and show off the car. His skin colour never got past green (for envy) right through the morning. The conversation was strained to say the least. He knew I'd just had the new car delivered, but never once asked to look at it (it was sat right outside the café window so it was hard not to look). Nor did he comment or congratulate me. When we left the café he nearly tripped over himself trying not to see my new motor. It was sad and perplexing, but a good reality check for me warning of things to come. It hasn't put me off aiming high; I still stretch for the stars, more so now than ever because I am better at it, but the blinkers are off. I keep my eye on the goal but at the same time I am ever aware of the events that will unfold when I achieve my aim.

Coffee break.

So what are the consequences of success? Who will it affect? What will it affect and moreover can you handle it? It all starts with desire, when this is strong enough intent is born and when that magic word comes into the equation, miracles start to happen. Events unfold to bring your goals into realisation. Intention – when laced with a passion that is prepared to risk even extinction on its realisation – creates a centripetal force that draws, magnet-like, all the ingredients that are needed to make your dream happen. It is a miraculous and awe-inspiring unfolding that never ceases to astound me. I love it. I love writing about it (especially when my desk is the deck of a Caribbean cruise liner, my own dream made manifest).

Hurdles and Pitfalls

There's more than one way to overcome hurdles.

The first thing intention triggers is a map to your destination, complete with all the obstacles that litter the path. Unfortunately, this is where many give up on the journey before it has even begun. They look at the obstacles and say, 'This is impossible, there are so many things in my way.' Remember that it is not in achieving your goal that you grow as a person and develop that elusive millionaire mentality, it is on the journey. The end, or goal, is very important on the journey, in fact it's vital, otherwise where are you going other than in circles? But it's the journey that is important in the end. And if your journey is littered with hurdles and pitfalls, if the obstacles are knee-deep then I say, 'Brilliant'. Brilliant because the more hills you climb, the stronger your legs will become, in fact without the hill there is no climb. I want obstacles, I thrive on them because it is exactly and entirely these 'impediments' (as people wrongly see them) that are going to make me the gentle giant I want to become. Do you think Messner, the greatest mountain climber in the cosmos, would have wanted to climb Everest if he thought it wasn't going to stretch him to and beyond his limits? Do you think he'd have wanted the Nanga Parbat (an 8,000 metre mountain in Pakistan) title under his belt if it were not deemed as impossible to climb alone? I think not. His climb was arduous and at times he didn't just feel like giving up, he felt like dying, in fact it took him three attempts before he succeeded in reaching the summit. Here is a brief extract from his book *Solo, Nanga Parbat* to show you exactly what I mean. It's important because we tend to look at others who succeed in life and imagine that their dreams came without the struggle.

I have climbed a steep section of the mountain [Nanga Parbat] and now, breathless inside my tent, the realisation hits me that I cannot get back down again. I lie rigid, unable to move, and am sweating profusely even though it is so cold. Hoar frost coats the drab fabric above my head. I mutter to myself, call out, yet cannot hear the sound of my own voice. Panic has me in its clutches and all I want to do is scream.

It came suddenly upon me in a moment between sleeping and waking when I was pondering the route ahead. In a moment I saw just how alone I am. So alone. The muscles in my stomach tighten with fear.

I am a speck on this vast mountain face, I cannot see back to the start of my climb. Below me the dizzy void has no end.

Within seconds terror has reduced me to a weak, shivering bundle, I want to crawl away and weep, and never, never have to look down again. My fingers will no longer grip; my legs no longer support my weight. I want to close my eyes but they remain open.

Despair at being alone floods my whole body. Fear of being here, fear of going on, fear of being alive even.

This is sheer madness, I say to myself; I'll give up.

But of course he didn't give up, he never gives up. Now I have never climbed Nanga Parbat, but I have climbed my own personal mountains, and so many times I have felt like giving it all up. That's why I love this opening paragraph to Messner's great book. If this legend, this god, can be scared to the point of weeping for his wife then it's OK for me to be scared too. And being scared doesn't mean that I will not make the peak, I can make it not just in spite of my fear, but because of it, I can use the fear as a fuel.

So it has to stretch you, it is the stretch that makes you bigger.

I can't imagine Mr Messner sitting with his other mountaineer buddies saying, 'There's this mountain right, well it's more of a hill actually. Did I say hill? I meant a very large mound of mud. Anyway, I've heard that it's a cinch of a climb; you don't even get a sweat on. Though I did hear that some guy broke a toenail climbing it last year. What do you reckon? Shall we do it?' His mates would have taken the lad (right away and right enough) to the local trick-cyclist for a neck-up-check-up.

Messner didn't just look for mountains with a giant-slaying reputation; he looked for impossible-to-climb peaks that had killed other would-be conquistadors. When he climbed Everest, he knew that this mountain was littered with the bodies of previous climbers – which is why he wanted to climb it – then he added more pressures on himself by deciding to scale it without oxygen. Six weeks after conquering this beast (actually he never felt like he'd conquered this or any other mountain, he felt like he'd sneaked up whilst it wasn't looking), Messner, for the third time, attempted (and succeeded) to climb Nanga Parbat solo. A feat never accomplished by another living human.

The point I am trying, perhaps labouring, to make is that ordinary people look for an easy climb in life; consequently they never hit the big peaks. The champions only climb the easy peaks in preparation for, and for a better vantage point of, the big peaks.

Again, backtracking a bit, there is nothing wrong with the small hills; we need them to build the right mentality to do the higher ones. You don't attempt Everest if you're out of breath climbing your stairs at home. But at some point, you have to recognise the fact that to get the best fruit you have to climb to the top of the tree.

So it's all about perspective. To succeed, you have to look for and welcome the obstacles, because adversity precedes height. No adversity, no advance.

My friend rang me and said, 'I've just been awarded my 1st Dan black belt in kung-fu – by post.'

'How so?' I asked, a little confused.

'Well,' she continued, trying to rationalise it as much for herself as for me, 'there's this company in America that will grade you if you send a tape in of your technique.' The phone line went quiet.

'How much did it cost you?' I asked, knowing that the amount would be substantial. She told me. It was. After another uncomfortable pause she asked the question I knew would come.

'Do you think it was worth it?'

Rather than answer a question that was leaked with doubt – the fact that she had to ask my opinion in the first place hinted that she doubted the worth of her new grade – I asked a question in return. 'How was the journey?' She'd arrived at port 1st Dan and I wanted to know if the journey was a difficult one and whether getting there had given her a 1st Dan mentality. I wanted to know about the adversity that she'd faced, the obstacles that had tested her to the absolute limit. Did she lie on the bed and cry (I did when I was going for my brown belt in shotokan) because she doubted her ability to handle it, did she get to the point of wanting to give it all up, did she doubt her very existence, did she reach the 'Messner point' of being so low that even life itself frightened her? She thought for a second. 'I was a bit nervous when I sent the tape off,' she said. Another pause, 'No not really,' she concluded. I didn't need to say anything else.

I'm not judging this very lovely friend. When I was younger, like many people, I tried to get ribbons without running races – and occasionally, like this lady, I did. But never, without exception, did I get any higher up the hill just because someone gave me a certificate saying that I did. It's a hard lesson to learn. This is a reciprocal universe, what you put in is what you get out.

So if the path is beaten and smooth with a distinct lack of rocks, there is a fair chance that this is a path well travelled by the masses, by the 95 per cent who are looking for an easy hike – which is great if that's all you want. You need to be on a different path, one less travelled, in fact if you want big time then look for a path not travelled at all. Don't be discouraged because of the obstacles, be encouraged, and be excited by them because the road to Damascus lies before you.

The Magic

The first thing providence does when you plug intention into the mains is to say, 'This is what you ordered (the goal) and this is what it costs (the journey).' It's like a reality check, it's like the wholesalers ringing you up and saying, 'Mr Thompson, we have an order here for enough seed to cover ten acres. We are very grateful for the order, but we are a little confused. You only normally order seed for one acre. Seed for ten is available to you, but it will cost ten times more. Are you sure the order is right?' This is your 'cool-off' period, your moment of reflection and your chance to see the mountain before you attempt the climb. The wholesaler (the universe) is not saying, 'You can't have this,' or even, 'You can't handle this,' it is simply saying, 'Can we just check your order and show you the cost, just in case you were not aware. Just in case you ordered incorrectly.'

When I order from Amazon.co.uk they always show me (at the checkout) what I have ordered and what it will cost, even how long it will take to arrive. At the bottom of the screen is a little button that says: cancel order. No hard feelings, no gloating because you may have bitten off more than you can chew. Just a button to let you off the hook, no questions asked. The universe is the same (only a little – not much – bigger than Amazon). When you place the order it shows you the cost before you start, so you can look at the order and say, 'Can I really afford this? Can I really do it? Is it really what I want? What am I really prepared to pay to make this happen?' The great thing with this, the beautiful thing, is that sometimes you look at the cost (you may even be part way into the journey) and say to yourself, 'Actually, I don't want this at all, not at any cost,' which is great. It is an avenue you thought led to gold, but it actually led to brass.

I had a friend who wanted to join the 23 SAS. He thought he wanted it with all his heart. He made getting into this elite unit his intention; in fact, he made it his life, to the exclusion of everything else, including his long-term girlfriend. He made it through to the selection, a lengthy and extremely testing process, before he realised that his dream, his expectations of what being an elite soldier was, did not match up to the reality. He knew he could finish the selection, he was fitter than the very fittest of butchers' dogs, but suddenly he didn't want to. His adversity, the selection, had brought him a goal of a different kind, one that he'd not envisioned on his initial game plan. He realised that his lady – the one he was losing at a rate of knots – was the most beautiful girl on the planet and that the world he was leaving behind, far from being a dull nine-to-five existence, was a kicking life and he wanted it back. It wasn't too late, so he left the selection with a backpack of new dreams, new goals that to him were worth ten Special Air Service Caps.

As I said, success is extremely subjective, one man's fantasy is another man's factory. The Universe often does this. Like

Amazon, it gives you a glimpse of what you pay for your goals, and you may think, 'How much?' and promptly cancel the order.

I had an American gentleman ring me recently from Massachusetts. He wanted to place a substantial order with me for books and videos. Even with very generous discounts, his order still came to a large amount. I sensed a little hesitation in his voice, but he still proceeded to complete the order without pressing the cancel button. An hour later I walked into my office. There was a message on my answer machine from the American gent. 'You know,' he said (you have to imagine this in an American accent), 'you know Mr Thompson, I just checked my credit card statement and I think I may have been a little over-ambitious when I ordered every book and video you ever produced. My balance will not allow me to proceed with the sale right now. I'm sorry for any inconvenience I may have caused. When my balance is better, maybe next month, I'll be back to place a smaller order.' Isn't that great (no, really!) I loved this guy's attitude. He was saying, 'I want your products (or his goal), I want them a lot, but at this moment in time I don't want (or I cannot afford) to pay the price. But next month I think I'll have the means to make a smaller order, one I can afford!

When you intend for something to happen, the first thing it lights up is the cost. Do you want it and can you make the payments? It gives you the chance to have a cold hard look at what you are getting into. If you look at it and say, 'Yeah, that's OK, I can deal with that,' you are on your way. The plane, as they say, is about to leave the runway. Intention is very powerful, especially when charged with passion, so much so that in your mind's eye it is already a reality. If I focus, if I concentrate my energies on to any goal, *any* goal, I believe I can make it happen. Frightening! No really, my creative power (our creative power as a species) is scary. I remember wanting to get into the Royal Court Writers Group in the West End of London. It is the most prestigious group and the most exciting theatre for new writers in the world and I wanted to be in it. I wanted it for two reasons. Firstly, so that I could confirm my belief that I was a good writer and secondly, because I wanted help in developing my writing skills. I set my sights on the Royal Court Theatre because they, I felt, were the best people to do both. Some of the best writers in Britain started out at this very theatre. My favourite playwright, Jim Cartwright, being one and the very funny and brilliantly talented novelist/playwright/all round superstar, Sue Townsend (of Adrian Mole fame), being another.

My desire quickly became an impassioned intention and I set to work on my first play. It was a big jump from books to plays, especially considering that I went right for the summit in one fell swoop. I spoke to my friend on the phone, 'I've written a play,' I told him. 'I've sent it to a theatre.'

'Great,' he replied. 'Which one?'

'The Royal Court,' I said proudly. The phone went quiet, 'Are you still there?' I asked.

'The Royal Court in the West End?'

'Yeah.' Another pause, 'Why?'

'Well,' he said, like it was going to be a revelation to me, 'that's the top theatre, probably in the world for new writers!'

'I know,' I said. 'That's why I sent it there.'

As is usual, reality gave me the cost printout, letting me know what I'd ordered and the price in advance. Did I want to proceed? The cancel button was at the bottom right of the screen if I decided not to. Wow! The cost was a lot higher than I had envisaged. I'm a fast writer, I can knock out instructional books in a week, and I figured that the cost might be some very hard work, for maybe a month. And I may have to stretch a little. I could handle that.

I had made the mistake that many make. I had watched a couple of plays on stage and thought, rather arrogantly, 'I could do better than that!' Not realising of course that saying and doing are two entirely different things. I've even had the audacity to do the same with books, 'I could do that, it's dead simple!' Oh yeah? Let me tell you, writing 'simple' is an art form perfected by only a very few.

One guy rang me up to tell me that my books 'are not bad' (implying 'not that good either') and that he was going to write similar books, but with more in them! The implication was that he could, and was about to, do better. Also, he asked whether he could send his work to me to look over? 'No problem,' I said (this is my standard response), 'send it down.' I was not offended (much). I've fallen into the same trap many times myself. By the way, I've yet to receive a finished job from the ones that say it's easy!

In reality, this supposed one-month task meant over a year of work on one play. A year of pulling teeth without anaesthetic. Twelve months of writing, polishing, re-writing, re-polishing, then again, and again (until infinity and beyond). Then there was the doubt. Could I really deliver the goods, could I really write at this level, would they laugh at my attempts to become a playwright, would they send back the work, still in the same envelope with a standard 'not in this lifetime you loser' rebuttal that might garrotte my dreams of ever seeing my words leave the lips of A-list actors? Once the work was done, then came the wait, and what a wait. Months with nothing. Then the doubt again, and defensive anger, 'Why can't they just look at my work and give me an answer? How long does it take to read a play?' Little did I know at the time that the Royal Court receives thousands of manuscripts a year, and that each script is read and reviewed by several experienced readers. Only a few get through.

When I finally did get the call to say that they liked my work I was overwhelmed. I had aimed high, and hit home, but was struggling to handle my success.

All of a sudden Sharon and I were sat in the Royal Court Theatre, being told by Graham that I had (he felt) a distinctive voice for stage. I had an original voice and they wanted to help me develop it in their workshops, with some of the best writers, directors and producers in the business. I was there. I had arrived and it depressed me. It was too big to fit into my head and it made me feel down. I kept saying to Sharon, 'So what does it mean?'

'It means,' she said very patiently, (I had been asking the same question for two days), 'that they think you've got a great voice for theatre.'

'Do you think they mean it?' I wasn't fishing for compliments, just trying to fit this chunk of success into a mind that was still at first base.

'Geoff, they don't have time to humour people. If you didn't have it (the elusive 'it' that everyone seems to be searching for) they'd have got rid of you post-haste.'

'So what does it mean then?' Sharon looked exasperated, so I shut up for a while. After two days of feeling low, despite my obvious success, I remember lying on the bed, a cartoon doom-cloud suspended above me. I asked myself again, 'So what does it mean?'

A kindly voice, one that I didn't recognise as my own said, 'You wanted it, you got it. Now deal with it.'

I remember thinking, 'Yeah, I did ask for this, and I did want it, so much so that I made it real.' That's what frightened me. The fact that I, the kid from the factory, the man from the nightclub doors of Coventry, the factory cleaner, had made a miracle and moved the proverbial mountain. I did it. I had some help, sure. I was guided by visible and invisible friends definitely, but I was the one that had taken the thought (I want to be in the Royal Court Writers Group) through to its physical manifestation. At this point I realised I could do anything, go anywhere, and be anyone. We all can.

I was born to succeed; we all are, though we perhaps do not fully realise this.

Battles

Sometimes in life we face adversity, we experience personal or professional problems. We have battles and, at the time, they often seem huge. We wonder if we'll cope. But really, if you think about what we have already been through just to be born, our life problems are minuscule in comparison. The goals we set ourselves that sometimes seem impossible are really not as big as we allow them to become. In fact, compared to surviving the fight for life they are pretty insignificant and very, very achievable. When you consider our individual uniqueness, the fact that we are each a totally original one-off, tailor-made human being, you realise that we really were made to win. There is a billion years worth of genetic information in our bodies – information passed on to us by our ancestors since time began – that wants us to excel, that compels us to grow, to explore, to stretch, to achieve. It is there to help us take the species to a place it has never been before (I don't know the destination, but I am looking, and I will drop you a line or write you another book when I find out). There has never been anyone quite like you. And there never will again. Some people feel like they are born losers, like life has it in for them and that the world is somehow against them. Please! Look at what you've achieved this far, look at the billions upon billions of cells that make up the person in your bathroom mirror and realise that you have already been fabulously successful in the business of humankind. You have taken one tiny cell and successfully invested it, with a return that is many times more than the initial investment. You were born to win. Do the same with a penny and you'll be a millionaire, invest one cell of love into others and you'll make a million friends (and very big phone bills).

As Napoleon Hill and W. Clement Stone in their wonderful book *Success Through A Positive Mental Attitude*, point out, just think:

Tens of millions of sperm cells participated in a great battle, yet only one of them won – the one that made you! It was a great race to reach a single object, a precious egg containing a tiny nucleus. This goal that those sperm were competing for was smaller in size than the point of a needle, and each sperm was so small that it would have to be magnified thousands of times before it could be seen by the human eye. Yet it is on this microscopic level that your life's most decisive battle was fought. The head of each of the millions of sperms contained a precious cargo of twenty-four chromosomes, just as there were twenty-four in the tiny nucleus of the egg. Each chromosome was composed of jelly-like beads closely strung together. Each bead contained hundreds of genes to which scientists attribute all the factors of your heredity. The chromosomes in the sperm comprised of all the heredity material and tendencies contributed by your father and his ancestors; those in the egg nucleus the inheritable traits of your mother and her ancestors. Your mother and father themselves represented the culmination of over two billion years of victory in the battle to survive and then one particular sperm – the fastest, the healthiest, the winner – united with the waiting egg to form one, tiny living cell. The life of the most important living person had begun. You had to become a champion over the most staggering odds you will ever have to face. For all practical purposes you have inherited from the vast reservoir of the past all the potential abilities and powers you need to achieve your objectives.

You were actually born a champion, and no matter what obstacles and difficulties lie in your way, they are not one-tenth so great as those that have already been overcome at the moment of your conception. Victory is built into every living person.

The odds then are irrelevant if your intention is to succeed. But like the sperm looking for the egg you have to want it, and be prepared to battle for it with every sinew of your person.

Can you imagine a little sperm sitting watching sperm TV and scoffing his face saying, 'If I'm lucky I might get to fertilise the egg one day.' He's sat there waiting for the egg to 'come' to him (for want of a more – or less – appropriate expression), not realising that 'it ain't ever gonna happen!' You want a piece of the (metaphoric) egg, you'd better get in some swimming practice, get a few muscles on them sperm shoulders or you're going to be right at the back of the queue come fertilisation time.

Intend it to happen and write down your intention. There is no luck necessary other than that which intent manufactures.

Ask, ask, ask!

Like Providence, people wait for luck. Forget it. Make your own luck. It's amazing how much it will 'just happen' once you start the journey with a strong intent. The magic, let me tell you, is a wonder; it's exciting to see the miracle of creation in action. All the things you need, all the semantic details necessary to make the jigsaw into a complete picture will come to you as and when you need them. Don't be surprised when the phone rings and you are talking to Providence. Don't be too shocked at the serendipity that occurs when you meet exactly the right people or read the exact paragraph in the perfect book that will tell you how to get past a particular problem.

I remember one occasion, en route to a difficult ideal, when I closed my eyes and said, 'I could do with some advice if you get the chance.' It's amazing what you get when you dare to ask. Within a very short time of asking I was in a bookshop looking at books on sport. To my surprise, right in the middle of the sport section was a book on philosophy. I was surprised because the book was on the wrong shelf and in the wrong section of the shop. I picked it up and leafed through the pages and read a paragraph on a random page.

As I mentioned, I was stuck at a major stumbling block on my current goal-hunt. There were two questions in my mind that needed answering before I could proceed to the next stage. The first paragraph I read (at random remember) addressed this problem directly and told me exactly what I needed to know. I was delighted. Excitedly I picked another page and another random paragraph. This too answered a question, the second that I had been struggling to find an answer to. I bought the book and took it home to read and whilst the rest of the text was good, it did not tell me a single other thing that I needed to know at that particular time. The two things I did need to know were found miraculously at random and for no cost. All I had to do was ask with the expectation that it would be answered. Is it God that answers? Is it a providential angel? Are we tapping into a bank of intelligence where all the answers lie waiting for curiosity and goal-seekers? Could it be that in asking we are triggering one of the billions of genetic information cells locked into our brains waiting for the key holder to access the lock? Do the answers come from your higher self? I suspect it is all of the above.

Ask, ask, ask. Stuck on a problem? Why not ask for help. Why not go to the collective and invisible library, get the key out and ask.

So many people say to me, 'I don't know how to . . . ' (You fill in the gap).

Ask!

How many times do people say, 'If only I knew . . . '?

Ask!

What have you got to lose? But once you do ask look out for the answer or you might miss it. As one of the great books (the Bible) advises: *Ask and you shall receive, seek and you will find, knock and it shall open unto you.* The key? Ask!

It was only very recently that I found myself with another difficult problem. Actually, *I* was the problem. I let my guard slip and found myself down Angry Street. A place I have not visited for many years. A place I'd said I would never visit again because the buildings and the people are ugly and unpalatable. Let me tell you very briefly (have you got a couple of hours?) what happened. Actually, I'll tell you in a moment if you don't mind; the sun is just rising over the horizon and I don't want to miss it. A family of dolphins has been following us for half an hour and the Island Margarita is just honing into view (and my coffee cup is empty). I am about to get a decaff refill and I'll be back in just one paragraph. Please excuse me.

I'm back. The coffee, I have to tell you, is hot, there is a warm breeze drifting across from my left and a motorway of sea cut out to the rear of the ship as far as the eye can see. Other passengers are joining me on deck now, it's nearly 6.30 a.m., breakfast is cooking and a brand new day is emerging around me. So where was I? Oh yes, Angry Street.

I'd had a small problem with my web page. My server had been quite awkward for the year I had rented web space from him, so I'd decided to move my page to another location. I did it properly. I waited until my year's contract had expired, gave the fellow written – and very polite – notice that I had decided to move my page elsewhere and then waited for him to release my tag so I could move to greener pastures. No answer. A week, two weeks, then three. 'Oh well,' I thought, 'the page is still on-line, and he'll release my tag in his own time.' Then I started getting calls, 'Do you know your site is down?' I checked on my computer and right enough the chap had taken my page off-line. The whole idea of me asking for an early release of my tag was so that I could move the site with minimal fuss. Maybe a couple of hours off-line, tops. Two weeks later, after dozens of unanswered emails to the company in question, and a plethora of phone calls that were met with the impersonal response of an answer machine, I still hadn't heard from him. And my site was still off-line. But I was still hanging on to my temper. Every day the page was off-line I was losing money, so my patience was wearing thin. Actually, I should come clean here. This wasn't about money, it was about my pride. 'How can he do this to me? Me!' I was hurt because I felt this guy was being hugely disrespectful and I was *that* close (I'm making a very small gap with thumb and forefinger, to signify just how close) to getting in my car and paying him a visit to make him release my site. We're talking about the introduction of 'physical' here – I was about to get physical with his throat. I wanted to shake the lad within an inch of his life and force him to give me what was mine. Sharon kept me calm, 'Don't worry,' she said, 'just keep contacting him, he'll release it soon enough, it's not in his interest to do otherwise. It's his karma, Geoff, don't allow it to become yours by making threats.' I have (after working as a nightclub doorman in a violent city for nine years) renounced violence in all its forms and I was determined not to take a retrograde step. Then something happened – and I must be clear here, I allowed it to happen – this particular gentleman placed a sign at the front of my page (or where my page should have been) saying, in not so many words, that my site was off-line due to 'breach of contract or non-payment of rent'. I was so angry, so angry.

Again I must reiterate here, I remember the exact point I allowed this minor problem to enter my mind and become major. It was when my friend, very well-meaning, said, 'You can't let him do this to you. We should pay the lad a visit and teach him a lesson.' I allowed a small seed of anger into my mind and within seconds it grew to monstrous proportions. I was fuming. I got on to my computer and with my friend at my shoulder, wrote an angry and threatening email. But when I pressed send, it wouldn't go. I said to Sharon, 'It won't send.'

'It won't send because it is wrong,' Sharon said. Then I tried again and my whole Outlook Express went down. I was so angry that I had crashed my computer.

Now, I believe that within every one of us are trillions of little electrical cells and that consequently we have the power to interfere with electrical equipment. My anger, my ill-channelled energy, had crashed my computer. My intent was very strong, but it was also very wrong. Providence was giving me a cool-off period. It was saying, 'Do you really want this goal? Do you really want the karmic bill that will fall through your letter box?' I was still very angry and hurt. Sharon, my angel, said, 'It's alright Geoff, we did OK without the web page before, we can do it again!'

'But,' I replied, 'we can't let him do this, if I don't go around and throttle him, how am I going to get my page back?'

'I don't know,' she replied honestly. 'But I do know that the price you want to pay is too much, I thought you'd left all that behind you.'

She was right. I looked at my friend and said with certainty, 'I've made a mistake here. I am never going to be violent again, unless my life depends on it. I will explore every legal means to get my site back, but I will not resort to violence, not even verbally, ever again.' I had decided, but I still felt angry and confused. My way forward seemed unclear. When you haven't got all the information, I have always believed, all you need to do is ask for help (and this is the crux of the story) and have faith that your prayer will be answered. I went upstairs and lay upon my bed and closed my eyes. I spoke to Michael – my Guardian Angel – and said, 'I could do with some help here mate. I will not be violent or angry again over this matter. I promise that, but I could do with your help.'

The next day I woke with the belief that I had given over my problem to a higher force and that help would arrive. I looked at my mail and was stunned to see a postcard amongst the letters from a friend who had not been in touch for a long while. He was a very spiritual chap who always seemed to turn up when I needed him most. But the fact that he'd gotten in touch was not what amazed me; it was the fact that the picture on the front of his postcard was of the Archangel Michael. Delighted, I walked into my office. The red light was flashing on my answer machine. I had a message. When I pressed play, my friend from the day before (the one who said, 'I know what to do, we'll kill him!') spoke, 'Hey Geoff, just checked your web page. He's released your tag. Don't know what happened there.' I know what happened.

At this point, had I been inclined, I could have emailed the fellow in question and left a 'don't you ever do that to me again' message with the implied threat that I'd smash his spectacles if he did. After all he'd released my page and was not in a position to harm it any more. I didn't. Instead, I emailed him, thanked him for releasing my tag and wished him well in the future. I have to point out that this guy would have been an easy target if I'd decided to get heavy, hell, my sister could have done it. But I knew that this was a lower echelon choice and that it would bring its own karmic unfolding.

There is a consequence, seen or unseen, to every action. I chose high and got great results. Two things happened after I sent the email. Call it coincidence, call it luck, call it unconnected if you like. I know what I'd call it. The consequence that comes from hitting all the right buttons. Firstly my email system that I'd crashed and that no one seemed to be able to get back on-line, suddenly started working again. Secondly, two days before, a deal I was trying to cut had fallen through. It was worth about £5,000 to me. After I'd come off the email the phone rang. It was the £5,000 guy. He'd reconsidered and would like to do the deal after all.

As I write this line I am sat on deck, it's 7.30 a.m. and we have docked at Margarita. Pelicans are diving into the sea for their breakfast. Like us they are hungry – them for food, us for knowledge. When they dive into the sea they don't think,

'I wonder if there are any fish today.' They know there will be. They have faith in the fact that when they thrust their beaks into the water they will get their meal. There are enough fish for all that ask. But don't sit on the beach with your pelican buddies waiting for the fish to beach themselves, because you may be waiting a long time. So many people die hungry (metaphorically speaking) because they fail to ask, or to act on the advice that is given.

ASK. Then look for the answer, it may come in the most obscure way, but it will come.

So, to conclude this chapter, remember: Intention is the key; if you want something make sure that you are prepared for the cost and then if you are still sure *intend* it to happen. And if you don't know what you want (many people complain that they want 'something' but they're not sure quite what) then *ask*, and leave all avenues open for the reply – you never know where it will come from. It is very important that you know what you want from life, you need goals. Why? I'll tell you tomorrow, very early.

– Secret Two –

The Power of Goals

4 a.m. Curacao – 4 January 2001

If you are going to employ intent, then you need to be intent on something. Otherwise your intentions, all that power, is blowing into the wind. You are a powerful liner with all engines going, fully manned but with no known port on which to call. You need goals, you need destinations and dreams. In the Bible it says: *Without dreams and vision, we perish.* Don't worry for now about the logistics or the semantics of how your dreams will manifest, first let's just concentrate on the goal itself.

There was a very famous survey carried out many years ago in Harvard. Harvard is renowned as one of the top universities in the world, attended by the elite, the cream of society. The survey was really just a general series of questions that asked each and every student their views on a number of unrelated topics. The responses caused quite a stir amongst the lecturers, particularly to the questions:

1) Do you have goals?

2) Do you write your goals down?

When all the papers were gathered together and the answers logged, the lecturers were taken aback. Approximately 15 per cent of those surveyed had goals and of this small percentage (this was Harvard after all, a University that prided itself on having the top people in the country) only a handful actually took the trouble to write their goals down.

As I said, the lecturers were both surprised and disappointed, but at that time, the survey was shelved. Many years later, at a staff meeting, the survey was brought up by one of the lecturers. 'Why not,' he suggested, 'do the survey again to see whether the people we attract at Harvard today are any more or any less goal-orientated than they were at the time of the original survey?'

Someone else said, 'Well, if we are going to do that let's throw a bit of money at it and trace the students from the original survey and see how their lives unfolded.'

It was agreed. The money was raised and the original students were traced and asked: Did you achieve the goals you set as a student? And those that did not have goals at the time were asked: How did your life pan out?

Amazingly, they found that 95 per cent of those who had not set goals had not achieved anything significant and were not financially independent. Of the 15 per cent who had set goals, 80 per cent achieved them, and of those few that actually wrote down their life goals, all had achieved them and all were financially independent.

They likened people without goals to ships leaving the harbour without crew or destination. How can you get somewhere when you don't know where 'somewhere' is? You can't, you'll be lucky just to get out of the harbour without bashing into something. You can take the longest journey and bear the strongest storms if you can see a destination ahead of you. No matter how hard things get, you can look forward and say, 'There's a light ahead. We'll be there soon.' Can you imagine hitting a storm on the way to nowhere? The temptation would always be to find somewhere safe to sit out the storm, or to turn back. Disillusion soon sets in when you have no goal. So many people in life give up for this very reason. You need a goal.

The Cost

As I said earlier, we have to buy our dreams and there is a cost, for those that are not prepared to pay, fulfilment is never forthcoming. Rather than take on the cost (not realising that paying the price is what gives them the mentality to handle their dreams), they sit waiting for the goal to come to them, for providence to knock on their door, for fortune to make its way to them, but it rarely happens. Millions (monetary or otherwise) rarely come to those who do not have the millionaire mentality. Income rarely exceeds personal development. All you have to ask yourself when dreaming is: Am I prepared to become the type of person it will take to handle my goal?

I look at my friend Glen. He is in fabulous physical shape. He has the kind of body most men aspire to have. Lots of sinewy muscle and no fat (don't you hate that?), he's built like a gladiator. But of all the people that come to the gym to find a similar body, probably only 5 per cent end up looking like Glen. Why? Because the 95 per cent are not prepared to become the type of person they need to be to get that body. They don't want to pay the price. To get a great shape you need to chart the right course, then have the discipline and the staying power to stick to that course without deviating to the island of cake, or the port of 'beer and curry'. To build a body like Glen Smith, diet – the ultimate discipline – is the pre-requisite. You have to get your diet down to a fine art. Very few make it because the journey is too arduous. Certainly the early stages are hard, when you have to change the cake-and-cookie habits you've perhaps been indulging for your whole life. Then of course, there's the training, whenever I go to the gym I see people making all the right moves, but again it is not just about the sweat and strain of a hard workout. It's the detail, it's working on the finer points.

Setting the Right Course

It is easy to say 'set a course to where you want to go and you'll get there'. People set courses all the time and still fail to reach their destination. This is often because they inadvertently set the wrong course, and subsequently they end up at the wrong destination, or back where they started.

You might be working extremely hard (even too hard – overwork can send you backwards at a rate of knots) but are you working in the right direction? I remember the time I wanted to develop a brilliant osoto gari (it is a throwing technique in judo). I had watched good judo players perform the move, seen detailed illustrations in books and even watched demonstrations of the throw on instructional videos. With my limited knowledge I set about achieving my goal. I practised daily, and very hard. I have always prided myself on being a tenacious – even obsessive – trainer. I practised osoto gari thousands of times, to destruction in fact, but I was practising it wrong. My destination was set, but the course was way off. I became brilliant at doing osoto gari the wrong way. I could have made instructional videos on 'how not to do osoto gari'. Subsequently, when I sparred with other players, I rarely pulled the throw off. Then I went to train with Neil Adams, one of the best judo men on Planet Earth. He knew the right way to osoto gari. He looked at my technique, told me I was doing it wrong, and in altering one or two little things he altered my entire course and hey presto, I got it. In fact, because I had been given the right map, and wanted to get there enough, I reached my destination (perfection of osoto gari) in record time.

So make sure that you set the right course. If you don't know it, ask the right people, those that are already where you want to be.

The Danger of Goals

So goals are essential, we have established that much, but they can also be dangerous. When you set goals, when you fully intend to make them happen, there is an inherent danger that you will achieve them. When you are fully determined, you are normally always successful. 'So what's the danger in that?' I hear you cry. The danger comes when you don't set your goals high enough. Sometimes we aim low and guess what, we hit low. And you could do so much more. Small goals are fine when they act as stepping stones to the higher goals, but in themselves, they can be very unsatisfactory. You end up thinking, 'Is that it?' You could, you know, have done so much better.

My friend Jane is a good runner. The other day she went out for a jog and she set herself a goal of five miles. She was capable of so much more, but she always sets herself this same achievable goal. 'Five is realistic,' she told me. 'I know I can do five, if I set more and don't manage it, I might fail and get disillusioned.' She set five miles on her internal clock and her body fuelled her up for the journey. By four miles she was flagging, by four and a half she was struggling and every step was an effort. She made five and was empty, though (she said) happy to have had a good run. She felt happy that she'd only run five miles because, 'I only just made that.' The next week, Sue, one of her friends at the running club, had to pull out of a ten-mile race and she asked Jane if she would take her place. Jane was hesitant, unsure if she could run ten miles, it was double her usual distance. 'Don't worry,' Sue said, 'just set your sights on ten, if you can't finish it won't matter.' Jane ran the race and killed ten miles and had a great time doing it. She injected necessity and the organism grew to compensate. She is now preparing for her first marathon. If you set your sights too low your body will automatically fuel you accordingly. If you were driving your car to the local city centre you would automatically only place enough fuel in the engine for the short journey. If however you had to make a very long journey you would automatically fill your tank to the top. Your body works similarly, if you set short distance goals it will fuel you accordingly, but if you set big goals it will fill your tank.

Paradoxically, I would say, 'Don't set your sights so high on the first shot that you become overwhelmed to the point of exhaustion.' Had Jane gone from a five-mile jog to the London Marathon (twenty-six miles) she might well have cashed a cheque that the bank could not honour.

So aim higher than you think you can manage, but not so high you lose sight of your goal.

The organism will grow to meet an injection of necessity. If you were a farmer with one acre, and you wanted ten, you could climb towards your goal in pyramidal steps. Perhaps start by acquiring another four acres. Knowing that five acres is too much for one person, you would hire some help, you could acquire more equipment to help tend the land, in fact everything would grow to meet the new demands. Eventually you could build up to ten acres.

Milo the Great

There is a wonderful story about Milo the Great, an ancient strong man whose goal was to carry a full-grown bull on his shoulders. 'Impossible,' all of his friends said. Milo knew different. He knew that picking a bull up at that moment in time was too much for him. He was strong mentally and physically, but carrying a bull was still too much for him. Instead, he bought himself a calf. Every day without fail, Milo would pick up the calf and walk around with it on his shoulders, and as the calf matured and grew bigger so Milo's strength automatically grew to compensate. Milo's legs grew in width and strength and his back and shoulder muscles expanded until he looked like a door wedge. Eventually, Milo – to the astonishment of all – could carry the full-grown bull on his shoulders. By picking up the bull as it grew, and subsequently pyramiding his own strength to match, he grew with the bull.

Your bull may not be a hairy creature with horns and a nose-ring (sounds like a girl I once dated – but that's another story) rather it might be your business, your college degree, it could be a promotional move at work, perhaps you are taking on a bigger mortgage – it could be anything. Like Milo, you don't have to pick up the bull right away and it isn't advisable to try, you should grow with it instead.

Ask any successful person whether they could have coped with their current position five or ten years ago. I recently taught an international seminar on martial arts in Las Vegas, Nevada for Mr Chuck Norris. Could I have taught the same seminar, with some of the most renowned martial arts experts on the planet, even five years ago? I don't think so. Five years ago, I would probably have filled my nappy because I was still teaching on a very localised level. I was lifting calves; a full-grown bull like this would have buckled my legs. Like Milo, I grew with the bull. I taught on a local level, then as my reputation (and subsequently my confidence and esteem) grew, I started to teach on a regional level, getting noticed by those on the national circuit. Eventually, I started teaching nationally and internationally. Then one day, I got a phone call from Richard Norton. Would I be interested in coming to Las Vegas, all expenses paid, to teach for Chuck Norris? (Does a one-legged duck swim in circles?) Even then, after the pyramidal growth from local to regional to national and international it was still a difficult step that I nearly never made (fear that the bull might crush me), but I did it and it was very successful; I stepped on to the world stage.

So picking up the bull for Milo was done in pyramidal stages. He used short-term goals (picking up the calf every day) to vehicle him to his long-term goal. Short-term goals are the rungs on the ladder to the top, they lead to long-term ideals.

You could use the same principle to buy the house of your dreams. Lots of people have secured fabulous homes by using the calf/bull principle. They start by buying a small property, selling it on and using the profit, and their savings, to move up the ladder to a bigger house. Eventually they manage to secure the home of their dreams. A couple I know used this method to take themselves, over a period of fifteen years, from a two-up-two-down terraced house to a beautiful property in three acres with a lake in the back garden.

And they did it on ordinary incomes. He worked as a window fitter and she stacked shelves in a supermarket. It can be done. Hard work? No harder than working your nuts and bolts off with no goal to aim at. Now I'm not saying that this is the only way. You can jump steps, you can go more than one rung at a time, but when you do the risk rises proportionately. It's all down to how much risk you can take. Some people crumble when danger comes on board. Others thrive on it and might go straight for the bull.

Pick up the calf every day until it becomes a bull. This way you hardly notice the extra weight.

Goal Pyramid

You could even build a goal pyramid to chart your steps from short-term to long-term goals. Mountaineers do this to allow themselves recuperation and acclimatisation to new heights. They make their way firstly to a base camp, acclimatise, then, step by step, they climb to the peak of the mountain, stopping regularly and setting up camp. When they get within reach of the peak they rest, eat, acclimatise and then, when the weather is at its best, they attempt the peak. It is all done in pyramidal steps. They set themselves daily goals, aiming to climb a set amount by nightfall. If the weather is clement they may (and often do) exceed their quota; on really bad days when the weather makes it too dangerous to climb, they may only make half the quota, or none at all. In which case they stay in the tent and rest up. Think of your goal as climbing a mountain. That is how Messner climbed Nanga Parbat.

I remember my mum placing my dad on a diet and him losing a couple of stone, so gradually he hardly noticed. My dad was carrying a belt-busting belly that was getting unhealthy (and unsightly) but he wouldn't hear of going on a diet. His self-discipline wasn't up to the job. My mum, worried about the dangers to his health, very gradually started to cut his dinner size down a tiny bit at a time and over a long period. Before he knew it he was eating light and healthy meals and looking and feeling good.

5.15 a.m. Cruising toward the island of Aruba – 4 January 2001
I have just refilled my decaff. 'Nirvana,' is all I can say. I was up at 4 a.m. writing and watching the sun come up and I can't think of anywhere in the world I would rather be right at this moment in time. Sharon is asleep in the room; she'll be joining me very soon for breakfast and then a day exploring this heavenly island. Life is good.

Let us get back to the book. The true purpose of goals, the real value of setting them is not, as you might imagine, in their achievement – getting or arriving at our destination is secondary. The major reason for setting goals that test and stretch you is to compel you to become the person it takes to achieve them. The greatest value of, let's say, becoming a millionaire is not the fact that you own a million quid, the greatest benefits to you (to us as a species) are the skills, the discipline, the information and the leadership qualities you'll have to develop to become a millionaire. It's the fact that you – and your whole world as a consequence – will change because of your journey.

I watched a documentary once about mountaineers and very briefly they spoke with an incredible guy who lives in a castle on a mountain somewhere exotic. He was like no man I had ever seen before. I didn't know who he was at the time, I'd never heard of him, but I knew that this man was *someone*. When he came on screen it lit up. He was a weather-beaten bohemian type, not a big man physically, with long hair and a character, what a character; his life was etched into every line on his face. I remember thinking, 'I want whatever it is this man has got.' It wasn't until years later that I found out just who this legend was and why he lit the screen the way he did. He was Reinhold Messner, the greatest mountaineer in history (as I may have mentioned before!). What he'd got, what he'd become, who he was, came from the fact that he climbed and conquered the hardest peaks in the world. Everest and Nanga Parbat to name just two. But what he had acquired along the way was not just a title, not just a photo on a peak or a mention in a record book. What he had/has transcends all of that. All of it. This man will carry his experiences, his journey, in his aura and beyond even death. His experiences are so profound that they will carry – via his genes and his inspiration – for generations to come. You wouldn't have to know that he had conquered previously unconquerable peaks to see he was someone, you wouldn't have to know or be impressed by any of his feats. You'd just look at him and know.

Gandhi was the same. You didn't necessarily have to know him to be awed by him. Spiritually speaking, he was a millionaire and he had the character of a giant even though physically he was very small. It was, by all accounts, difficult to be in his company without the experience changing you. The small man from peasant beginnings became a leader, wined and dined by Kings and Queens the world over. They wanted his company; they wanted a piece of him, a touch of what he had. But it wasn't just because this gentle man had achieved some amazing goals, it was because of who he had become in setting and achieving them.

Follow the Yellow Brick Road

In the film *The Wizard of Oz*, Dorothy and her troupe of mates are seeking a common goal, the Wonderful Wizard of Oz. They are seeking him because they believe he is the holder of their wants. Dorothy wants to go home to Kansas, the cowardly Lion wants to find courage, the Tin Man wants a heart and the Scarecrow is desperate for a brain. Each believes that when they find the Wizard in the Emerald City of Oz, he will simply give them, free of charge, their goal. Instead, he gives them a witch-finding task after which, he promises, he will grant each wish (even though he is aware that he is not actually in the position to do any such thing). He doesn't believe they'll ever come back; but return they do after accidentally killing the Wicked Witch of the East ('I'm melting, I'm melting,' you remember?). When they (completely unexpectedly) return to the Wizard – apparently not a wizard after all, just a balding old man behind a façade –

he gives the cowardly Lion a medal for courage, the Tin Man a heart-shaped watch and the scarecrow a university diploma. Whilst each believes they have been given their goal by the Wizard, in actuality they have, through their journey – first to Oz and then to find the Witch – earned their wants through their own efforts. On the journey the cowardly Lion develops courage by facing his fears and protecting his friends against the Witch and her army of mad flying-monkeys. The Scarecrow develops his brain by working out intricate game-and-fight-plans to find and then escape the witch, and the Tin Man develops a heart through a multitude of kind and charitable acts on the journey. What the Wizard gives them at the end of the journey amount to trinkets, symbols of their courageous quest. Their real goal started to manifest the very second they each agreed (intention) to seek their treasure. And because they had a solid intention the centripetal force drew all the help they needed; Glenda the Good Witch, the Wizard, the people of Oz, even the Wicked Witch helped inadvertently. As for Dorothy, the Wizard told her that the power to return home to Kansas was in her all along. Having killed the Witch (perhaps the symbol of her own negativity and her failure to appreciate what she already had at home), all Dorothy had to do was wear the Wicked Witch's magic red shoes and click the heels three times, whilst confirming and affirming that 'there is no place like home'.

We all have our own Emerald City to find and similarly we have to follow an individual Yellow Brick Road. When we have a strong intention that road will make itself known to us and all the help we need will come as and when we need it. That's what setting and achieving goals gives you.

So when you look at the final destination, from the safety of your mind's eye, ask yourself not, 'Am I willing to have this goal?' Ask yourself instead, 'Am I willing to become the kind of person it will take to get it?' Because who you become is far more important than what you get.

To conclude this chapter: set your goals, write them down and be clear that you are prepared to pay the price. And as a final note, remember never to mistake activity for progress. You could be the hardest worker in the land, but still not make your destination because you are going the wrong way. So how do you find the right way if you are unsure? Ask.

– Secret Three –

The Power of Asking

5.30 a.m. Somewhere very close to Venezuela – 5 January 2001
If I want to build a great body, if that is my goal, I'd need to cement my intention by writing it down. I'd also do well to write down the period of time that I intend to take to reach my goal. Writing down the time is important. If you place your order to be a bestselling author, champion golfer, successful painter, playwright, self-defence guru (or whatever) and do not write down a time limit (a date that can always be extended or shortened if you are not sure how long it will take), it hints that you are not totally committed to your goal. It suggests that fear has entered into the equation. Also it might mean that you get your goal, but not in the time that you would like it. It could happen years after you really wanted it to. If you are like my old self you might also fall into the fear trap. As a fledgling I would write my goal down, but never add a completion date. This was because I was scared of not making that date, of not completing my goal on time. I feared that by adding a date I was adding uncomfortable pressure. Deep down I was really scared of not making the goal at all. And by not making the goal, I had somehow failed, or even worse, that because I had failed to reach the goal, the 'process' (the law of 'ask and you shall receive') might be wrong. Maybe – I mistakenly thought – we don't have this creative inheritance after all; perhaps it's a lie. Doubt is a negative mental attitude, a weed killer that also kills flowers. Have complete faith in

your own powers and in the process and prove your faith by writing down a date of completion. It's OK to fear failure. It's natural at first to feel doubt, but weed it out with angry, determined focus and intention. 'I will make this goal come hell or high water, I will not let anything or anyone stop me.' This kind of determination makes mountains move. As I said earlier, the end is important at the start of your journey, but it's the journey that's important in the end.

Remember that it is not what you have, it's what you become. Determination, character, tenacity, courage, commitment, charm and focus are just some of the fruits of a hard journey.

Your goal needs a first step: intention. And don't worry sometimes if you slip back, we all do from time to time. That's why it is important to be around positive and empowering people, when you are around winners it is a lot harder to forget your way. How many times have you been really inspired and sprinted like a fast thing into a project only to find that, a short time later, you have lost the trail. It happens to us all. What I do, so as not to lose sight of where I am going, is to keep in touch with the books that inspired me in the first place. No end of times I have picked up a favourite book and re-read it, then thought to myself, 'How did I forget this stuff?' I had a great letter recently from a very successful and inspiring lady, Karen. She wrote, 'I have recently bought your book *The Elephant and the Twig*. I found it so inspirational that I have subsequently bought more copies for friends as Christmas presents. It is (to use your own words) "a kicking book". I could relate to the examples in your book; I left a safe job after 16 years and went back to college and not only did a degree but also my Masters as well. I have taught and worked in my chosen field but recently found myself slipping. I found a renewed optimism and courage from your positive examples and have followed much of the advice given (for instance, reading about the people I admire and realising how much more I need to read about them). When I find myself slipping (or being dragged) backwards I re-read your book. So . . . many thanks. Keep up the great work.'

So even very successful people need to be reminded (or need to remind themselves).

Going Blind is OK

Sometimes in life you just have to trust, listen to your instinct and trust. At this moment in time I am on a ship speeding through the Caribbean Sea; behind me, to the sides and in front, all I can see is black. Morning has not yet fully dawned and I can't see where we're going or even where we have been. For all I know we could be heading on course to nowhere. I haven't got any cast-iron guarantees, nothing is written in blood or set in stone. I don't know how this huge city of a ship works, how it can see its way in the dark, or even if there is anyone at the wheel but I don't need to, because that is not my job. My job is to intend my goal to happen (in this case a holiday in the Caribbean, on a boat at a set date and knowing the cost before I start). The rest is down to the captain. My captain is God (or Providence or whatever you want to call it). When I set my intentions in motion by writing them down and agreeing the price, I leave the details up to Him. My job is done.

Coffee is calling. The air is warm, the sea is rushing past us (I can't see it, but I trust it's there) and other passengers are starting to join me on deck. Only an hour to breakfast (I don't know the intricacies of cooking breakfast for several thousand passengers, that's down to the chef. All I know is I did put in my order). The coffee is kicking I have to tell you and all is well. I am at the aft (that's the back to all you landlubbers) of the ship with just a railing between me and thousands of miles of water. Below me it is three miles to the bottom of the ocean.

I was talking about commitment, about the fact that you should demonstrate yours by writing down your goal with a date of completion. As Susan Jeffers says so very well in her book *Feel the Fear – and Do it Anyway,* feel the fear of making that commitment . . . and do it anyway. Don't worry that you might not be able to handle it, tell yourself that you can (because you will).

When setting first-time goals it is easy to fall into the fear trap, it's easy to become overwhelmed. Later you will get off on being overwhelmed because it is the sign of growth, of stretching. But if you want the red apples on the high branches you have to be prepared to stretch. Don't settle for the ones that have fallen from the tree, they are bruised and old. Stretch, and when you do stretch, and acquire the (metaphoric) apple it will taste twice as sweet. I used to (in my days of crazy training sessions in the martial arts) run for five miles and then do anywhere between 20 to 30 three-minute rounds on the punch bag in my bid to become a world-renowned martial artist. Let me tell you that after my marathon sessions, a glass of cold water, a cup of tea or occasionally a cold beer, was nectar. The taste was beyond description. I earned that nectar.

When I worked on the building sites as a hod-carrier, it was backbreaking work, but the breakfasts, oh man! I can't tell you how good those breakfasts tasted. I earned that breakfast. When I was training in Birmingham with the wrestlers the workouts were amongst the toughest in my 30 years of martial arts. After two hours of being pummelled by the hard hands of Olympic standard grapplers, can you imagine how soft and silk-like my wife felt when I returned home at the end of the day. She was delicious. But, you see, I earned that delicacy.

So being overwhelmed is OK, and it doesn't last for long because your ability will grow to match your dreams. When you inject the necessity, the organism will grow to compensate. As the environment and the elements demand, you will grow to accommodate and cope. When I was first employed as a road digger, I did not have the physicality or mentality to cope with the harshness of the job. The summers were blistering and the winters brass-monkey cold. My body and mind grew to take in the hard workload and the harsh reality of roadwork. Even my humour changed to help lighten the punishing graft. Within a year I had a back like the side of a cow, Popeye forearms and a mentality to match. I was sharp with the piss-take and I had developed a thick skin because the piss-take coming back at me was savage.

This is the beauty, the magic of setting goals. The more you set, the more you will achieve and the more you will grow. The more goals you set, the more new opportunities will present themselves to you. Like a magnet you will attract providence, you will manufacture luck. When you attract luck and providence, have a guess what else you attract: people. Other folk. You become a people magnet because they want a piece of what you have and they are quite happy to pay – monetary or otherwise – for the privilege. Seemingly insolvable problems suddenly find their own solutions. Your belief system expands beyond measure and even greater goals come into view. Once you have a series of successes under your belt your confidence in the process flourishes and you start to believe – and rightly so – that nothing is beyond your reach. These successes act as reference points to further obstacles (or opportunities as you will come to see them).

Details please!

The sun has just arisen on the Caribbean Sea and way off in the distance I can see the lights of Curacao. The sea that I trusted to be all around me has lit up with the dawn as if to underline my faith, and the lights of a stirring island have confirmed once again my belief that the captain knows his way. It's his job after all. The breakfast bar is opening up behind me. I expected no less.

Intend your goals to happen and they will – like the sea, the island (and my breakfast) – materialise before your very eyes.

We have been talking about the fact that if you need help you should ask, and if you set a goal you should write it down. But if you are going to write it down you need to be specific. If you ordered a dress or trousers from a catalogue, you wouldn't write off and just say: Dress (or trousers) please. If you did, would you expect the warehouse to know what you meant? Or would you fill in an order form stating size, design, colour and amount? I am sure that you'd write the page number and the sort code of the very specific dress you wanted. If you didn't write the details you wouldn't expect the correct outcome. Can you imagine a warehouse with tens of thousands (millions or even billions) of items for sale and your order form says: Dress. The only thing you are likely to raise is an incredulous laugh. Your order would be returned to sender. At home you'd perhaps find yourself saying, 'This isn't a very good process, I ordered a dress ten years ago and it still hasn't arrived.'

So when you set your goals, when you ask, be specific. I remember standing in a service station on the motorway looking at the books for sale. I knew that to have your book in the service stations, railways or airports is a very big achievement in publishing terms because the latter only take the top-selling (maybe a couple of hundred out of a possible million) books. I looked at Shaz and said, 'One day . . . ' The implication was – though unstated and non-specific – that one day my books, or one of them, would be sold in the service stations, and therefore be a bestseller. My 'want' was passionate and I did write it down (note: I'm not saying that a goal not written down is a goal not achieved, rather I am saying that the very act of writing down the goal confirms your order). I wrote: 'One day (no date), one of my books (not which one) will be sold in every service station.' Massive intention, no detail. None. Anyway, I'd completely forgotten that I'd written this goal down in a non-specific manner, until one day I again found myself in a service station bookshop looking at the bestsellers. Sharon approached holding a fitness magazine (also on sale in the shop), 'Geoff,' she said with a wry and knowing smile on her face, 'you know your dream of having one of your books for sale in every service station?'

'Yes,' I said, very confused because she was talking books whilst passing me a fitness magazine.

'You made it,' she said and started laughing. And I had. Only not in the way I'd envisaged. I looked at the magazine. There, bold as you like, cover mounted on the front of *Men's Fitness* (a magazine I write a monthly column for) was a copy of one of my books. I'd sold an abridged version to the magazine in question and they had given it away free on the front of their magazine, as an enticement to buy. I had gotten what I had ordered, but not what I had wanted, in all the detail I should have asked for. I learned a lot from this lesson, not least the fact that the process works. I learned that you get what you ask for so make sure the detail is exact.

So ask in detail, how long, how high, when, where, how much of, size, colour and mode – you really have to define it. Remember: defined goals are like magnets.

One of my good friends actually carries a photograph of what he wants to achieve. He places it in his briefcase so that every time he opens the case he can see the goal in full-colour splendour. On one occasion he had a photo of the latest, top of the range Rover car in his case. At the time this was the car to have. He wanted the car in royal blue, but the only picture he could find at the time was of a racing green version of the vehicle. He didn't think it mattered too much. During one particular business meeting, he placed the photo in the back of his case out of view, he had to keep referring to notes in the case and the photo was in the way. After the meeting he forgot all about the photo and it remained hidden. About nine months later my friend received delivery of his dream Rover. And a beautiful car it was too. It wasn't until a couple of months later that he realised the power of detailed intention. He was clearing his case out and came upon the old photo, the one he had meditated and focused on every day. Then he compared it to the car sitting in his drive. It was the same in every detail. Even the colour. His new car was racing green. He'd wanted royal blue, but when he went to the garage to order his car they said they were clean out of blue, and would he accept one in racing green?

When David, a successful and now retired businessman, finally sold his business he signed the deal with the exact pen he'd seen in his mind's eye years before. When he sees his goal it is in microscopic detail. The make of pen, the colour, the feel of it as he signs his name, the touch of the paper in his hand, the smells, the sounds and the feelings. You get the picture. Detail is all-important because you get what you ask for. Getting a green Rover instead of a blue one is OK, you can live with that. But do you really want a dress in shocking pink, four sizes too small and in a style that does nothing for your hips? This would be a worry, particularly if you top the scale at 14 stone, have tattooed legs and you're accustomed to wearing trousers.

So, in conclusion: set your goals. *Ask* – but make sure you include all the detail because you tend to get what you ask for. Oh, one more thing, when you ask, when you set your goal make sure you know why you want it. You need a reason, it's very important. Why? Let me tell you in the next chapter.

It's 2 a.m., the moon is lighting up the sky, and the ocean is speeding past us chopping and slushing against the side of the ship. We have a 700-mile journey back to Barbados, and the second leg of our trip.

Sleep beckons; I go to bed with a very full day under my belt. It's been another great one.

– Secret Four –

The Power of Reason

6.30 a.m. Somewhere in the Caribbean Sea – 7 January 2001

One thing I have learned and one thing I know is that you have to have a reason for wanting to achieve a goal. People often ask me, 'How do I get from A to B or from B to C?' But the 'how' is not so important as 'why'? When you have the why, you will find the how. It will be sucked in by the centripetal force created by your own intention. If you have no reason you will, very likely, lose your way. You'll find yourself (when times are tough) thinking, 'Why am I doing this, why am I putting myself through this pain?'

Gandhi made himself a world leader and this one wonderful man triggered events that actually changed the course of history. He put himself through some major personal ordeals, but he had powerful reason. Many saw his race as third-class citizens, they were treated in many quarters no better than scavenging dogs. His goal was to change this and his reason was that he was no longer prepared to accept the ignorance of bigoted people.

William Wallace witnessed the atrocity of an entire Scottish village being raped and butchered by the English. He decided to do something about it. Like Gandhi, he dedicated his life to doing just that. One man changed the course of history. They make films about these people. And yet they are ordinary folk, like you and me, but with a reason so strong that even history records their daring deeds.

Following an individual path can take a lot of courage because it is always along the road less travelled. This can make it a very lonely path; the temptation is often to go with the flow of the crowds and seek company on Easy Street. En route we often take refuge from storms in safe harbours. At this moment in time I am on the seas of the Caribbean with its beautiful islands. I happen to know that when these islands were discovered by Columbus many of his sailors, after taking refuge before returning home, never left. They lost sight of their goal or in some cases they found a new one – staying on one of the paradise islands – and so they allowed a safe haven to become a permanent abode. As I say, this is OK if your journey shows you a better ideal than your original, but if it is not then take your rests, make your repairs and then move on. Don't allow a short rest to become a permanent sleep.

Go into any judo club – a notoriously difficult sport where the gradings for different belts are bone-crunchingly hard – and you will see lots and lots of practitioners wearing different coloured belts, but very few wearing the coveted black. The journey to black belt in judo is one of the most difficult, and thus revered, in the martial arts. The practitioners have to fight and win at public gradings for each colour belt. The grading days are long, hard and uncomfortable. The higher the grade you take the more fights you must have (and win). For the black belt itself, you have to win two matches by 10 points (Ippon, the highest point you can get in a judo contest) against others fighting for the same grade. Winning a fight is hard enough, but winning by ten points is very difficult. You can win the match by throwing your opponent clean on his back, pinning his back to the mat for 30 seconds or obtaining a submission via an arm bar, a strangle or through pure exhaustion. If you win two fights you qualify to fight in a line-up where you face three fresh opponents, one after the other with no rest. You have to win all three contests (again each by Ippon) to gain your black belt. Perhaps hardest of all is the fact that you are fighting other people going for the same grade and (in the line-up) if you beat them they automatically fail, if they beat you, you fail. When I took my black belt in judo, there were people attempting the grade for the fifth and sixth time. Getting the grade first time is extremely rare. I have trained with international fighters who took several attempts to secure it.

My point is this: every club you visit is full of people who are on different colour belts. Nothing too unusual in that you might think, until you realise that most of them have been stuck on the same colour for years and years, most never attain the end goal of black. Like many journeys, when the challenge gets uncomfortable, when the trade winds blow against them and storms attack, these practitioners seek sanctuary and a resting-place; they stop at an inn for the night to get out of the storm. One night becomes two and two nights three, and before they know what's happened, the inn becomes an abode and a permanent one at that. In the end they fear to leave.

Often our original goal – in this instance the black belt – is lost, forgotten or abandoned. If you stay at the inn for too long you start sprouting roots; you form friendships with, and seek solace in others who are in the same predicament. In your collective comfort-zone you sit and talk about how fierce the storm is and how hard the journey has become. It becomes difficult, often impossible, to leave because the periphery is a fence of fear that gets thicker and higher the longer you stay. People stay so long at the inn that they kid themselves – or they let others convince them – that this inn *is* the final destination, the goal. It's easier than picking the journey back up and certainly it is more palatable than admitting that they have given up. Hence when you go to any judo club you will see an abundance of people stuck on the same colour belt. The most common colour to get stuck on, interestingly, is brown, the penultimate belt, i.e. the one below black. You lose so many people in the martial arts in this final stage. They are within sight of their goal, they can see the peak, but all of a sudden the unfulfilled desire seems a lot more reassuring than the attainment of the goal itself.

They forget why they wanted the goal, or they aimed for the goal with no specific reason in mind. It is when the going gets really tough that a strong reason is probably the only thing that will pull you through. Recently I read in the paper about an elderly gentleman who had a life-long dream of making it to 100 years of age. His reason? He wanted to get a telegram from the Queen (a British custom) on his 100th birthday. And he did. On his 100th birthday he received the telegram congratulating him. He opened the letter, smiled and said, 'I made it.' Within a week he had dropped dead. He had given himself a strong reason to live to that ripe old age, but none to live beyond it.

So make sure that you have a strong reason, stop at the inn, yes; shelter from the storms and rest when rest is needed, absolutely, it's important that you do; but please pick the journey back up post-haste before you get roots-in-your-boots and your bottle puts up the white flag. It's hard! Yes of course, but it has to be hard. If the forge were only warm it would not temper the blade.

Why You Want Your Mind's-eye Goal

The 'why' is vital. There have been a number of times in my life when I've wanted something, whatever it was, but was never really sure why. Guess what? I didn't get it. In fact on a number of occasions I didn't even try. The reason was not there, the 'why' was not in place.

I find it so exciting that we can have anything, we can do anything, go anywhere and be anyone. I love that, don't you? The only minus (it's hardly a minus) is that we are spoilt for choice. Often we have so many options that in the end we don't choose at all. I call it the video syndrome. Have you ever gone to one of the larger video shops, but without a firm choice of film in mind (no goal)? I have, on many occasions, and nine times out of ten I come away with nothing. I find myself picking up videos, reading the back-cover blurb and then umming-and-erring. What if I get the film out and it's rubbish? The reviews are good, but reviews are very subjective. I get so frustrated that I end up with nothing. Some people, I know, will just go in and randomly take a film, working their way through the whole lot over a period of time. Again, nine times out of ten, the film they choose, for whatever reason, does not cut the mustard and the evening is spoilt. Setting a goal, even with a video, needs a choice and a reason. If I have watched a video preview, it gives me a taste of the film, so when my wife, my kids, or my internal dialogue asks, 'Why are you getting that film?' I can say I watched the preview and it looks like a great film, my kind of film, a film I'd like to watch; interesting, informative, educational, raunchy, whatever it is that cuts it for me. I can't imagine choosing a film without a reason.

Life offers us similar reviews of a given, chosen or desired goal. That's normally how we choose our goals. We see a review and think, 'I'd like that.' The goal could be a big house (or just a house), a Jaguar La Coultre timepiece, a Hugo Boss suit, a new language, or the ability to play a musical instrument. I always, for as long as I can remember, fancied learning a musical instrument. I wasn't sure which instrument, so I had no set goal and I didn't really know why I wanted to learn, so I certainly didn't have a good reason. Then last year I decided my goal would be to play the guitar for a definite though very simple reason – it'd be great fun and a nice way to relax. Once these two must-haves were in place, my goal happened very quickly. I mentioned to a friend that I had an interest in learning the guitar and he offered me free lessons, which I am still having to this day. And guess what? I now play guitar. Once I made the commitment, the magic unfolded. People gave me tips, advice, music sheets, Sharon bought me a new guitar, and Bill (my guitar teacher) re-strung it for me with metal instead of nylon strings. I even made a friend, Jason, at *Total Guitar Magazine*. He'd read and liked my books, heard that I was interested in the guitar and so sent me a bunch of back issues (complete with free 'learn guitar' CDs) and an invite to meet and 'talk guitar'. It's wonderful, but like a journey there needs to be a first step. You have to take action. You might have all the information, all the right tools, a map, you're even fuelled up, but for whatever reason you don't leave your driveway. Like many, you become a 'gonna-do-it' guy who wants, but never gets, because you put off the journey permanently with the 'one day I'm-gonna-do-it' statement that becomes your epitaph. Don't 'gonna-do-it', Just Do It! (As the ad says).

I'd say that a reason is not just important, it's imperative. As I said, when you hit inclement weather it is what keeps you on track. You can reach any height, and I mean any, but reason is going to be paramount. When the storms hit – as they invariably will – believe me you'll ask yourself, 'Why am I here?' And you'd better have a good answer otherwise you'll find yourself on the next boat home. No shame in that, other than the fact that it will be a shame you didn't plan for inclemency. You plan by making your reasons solid, and if possible, many. The reason is completely personal. Your reasons for making the grade will no doubt be completely different from that of other people. Even if they are aiming for the same goal. It doesn't matter what colour the car is as long as it is roadworthy. You want money? Give me the *why* and you will be given the *how*? Fame? No Problem. Why? Answer that and the How will appear like a rabbit out of a magic hat.

Money is a popular goal, but ask yourself why? And then ask yourself if you are prepared to become the person it takes to get money. You place your order for money stating how much, by when and why you want it, and you will automatically be given the cost to you. Do you still want to proceed? At this point, looking at the cost, you may think, 'I didn't want it that much, my reason is not strong enough, the risk outweighs the reward, the investment is greater (to you) than the return.' That's good, you know where you stand and it's easy to press 'cancel'.

On the other hand, you may (hopefully) say, 'Yeah that's OK. I expected that, let's continue.' Or even better, 'I want this (whatever your goal is) at any cost,' (as long as it is legal, moral, doesn't hurt others, etc).

My friend wanted to be a nightclub doorman. He'd seen the preview (one of his friends was a doorman of repute) and he liked the look of it. He'd even got a reason; working as a doorman would give him credence amongst his friends and family (or at least he thought it would). He asked my advice, could he make the grade? He thought he had got all the numbers to the combination. But, from the outside looking in, his reason was weak; it didn't have the legs to climb a potentially life-threatening mountain. The city he wanted to work in had experienced nine violent murders that year alone and the murderers would be the type of people he'd be facing on a nightly basis. The respect of your family and friends is a good ideal, but you don't have to risk your life to get it. That'd be like investing £100 for a return of one penny. The respect from family and friends comes from things such as courtesy, charity, love, consideration, gentleness, being unselfish and taking time out to be with them. All these things are an investment of time, an investment of self, not an investment that might get you killed.

He asked me whether I thought him capable of working as a doorman. I answered his question with a question. 'How would you feel about getting a phone call at three in the morning from someone threatening to kill your wife and children?'

He looked at me like I'd just kicked his favourite dog, 'I don't want that!' he replied with certainty.

'Then you don't want the door,' I said, 'because that (the threat) is potentially what the cost is going to be. It might never happen, but it could happen the very first night you work.'

He didn't work as a doorman, because when faced with the (possible/probable) cost, his reason was left wanting.

I worked as a nightclub doorman for a number of years. I asked myself a similar question before I entered the trade. 'Am I prepared to take on all comers?' My answer was an emphatic, 'Yes!' Because my reason – I had a life-sapping fear of confrontation that I wanted, needed and intended to confront and overcome – was so strong that it was worth the ultimate risk, death. No need for exaggeration here, three of my friends, all doormen, were murdered in violent attacks.

You need to know *why* you want to achieve your goal. If you don't know why, then ask.

Life is very mysterious, it has a habit of hiding answers to our questions in such a manner that they become apparent only to those inspired enough to look for them, or for those who have good reason to look for them.

When you want something enough you will move mountains in your bid to get it, the answer you need, the methods, the solutions to your problems will be revealed to you.

Reasons

The reasons for wanting to succeed are as varied as people are. Some of the most common reasons or motivators are our loved ones; the desire to be successful so that you can give them the very best. Perhaps, as a child growing up, your parents were not able to give you the best and so your life vow is to make sure that your children do not suffer the same hardships. What a great reason, what a way to motivate yourself when the going gets tough.

As a youngster I wanted to be a top martial artist. My greatest motivation was that I wanted to be able to protect my family (and myself) against violent people. At times the going was so tough that I'd lie on my bed and cry. But I still managed to make the next session. Why? Because I wanted martial skill with a passion that made me stronger than my fear, in other words, my motive, my reason, completely over-powered my fear. When things got messy I would bring to mind my reasons, these would drive me forward when nothing else could.

Charity is another great reason to achieve. What better way is there to help others than to make use of your wealth and/ or platform? Benevolence is a very honourable reason to push ahead when your fear wants you to slam on the brakes.

My own feelings are that we should all use benevolence as at least one of our reasons to succeed. At the end of the day you can have all the wealth the world has to offer, but it means nothing, not a dot, without people. People, helping them, loving them, healing them, is all. When you give to others you can change lives for better and forever. Men, like the wrestling great George Hackeschmidt, used their global platform to help others. He didn't set up a charity, he didn't save a village in India and neither did he save the rainforest (though these are all laudable goals), what he did do was to change people's lives for the better just by having time for them. He was aware of his platform, his fame, and the fact that one positive word from him could, and on many occasions did, literally alter people's lives for the better. If George told you that you had the power to move mountains you'd be racing for a shovel to get started. He was a fantastic athlete, but more than that, he was a fantastic man who always made time for others, he always went that extra mile for people.

Buddhists call this Buddhichita, the art of serving others. But you know what, the beauty of serving others is that, in doing so, you serve yourself (oh yes you do you old cynic). Ours is a reciprocal universe where all that you give is returned with interest. This law is like gravity, what you give is what you get. Isn't that incredible? Wouldn't you agree? Everything you give, you will get back with profit. So benevolence is fantastically profitable. There's only one (very small) catch. I say small, but if this one element is not in place it stops the process. Well it doesn't so much stop the process because, like gravity, it is an irrefutable law that must, and will, unfold. The catch is that when you give you must never expect or look for a return from the person you gave to. You must know that it will return (it could come from anywhere), but never expect it. The moment you expect a return from the person you have given to is the moment you set yourself up for disappointment. Because the very act of expecting return turns a charitable gift into a quid pro quo barter. So you are no longer giving anything at all. You are merely swapping one gift for another. If – often when – that gift does not return you feel cheated, you feel bitter, you feel let down and you feel used. Even the simplest gift, like opening a door for someone, backfires if you expect a return. I would often open the door for people only to be offended if they didn't thank me. I'd find myself sarcastically muttering (even shouting) to myself, 'Thanks for opening the door. Think nothing of it. My pleasure.' I kidded myself that I was a nice person because I opened the door for strangers. I told myself what a courteous fellow I was, but in reality, I was little more than trade swapping one lot of merchandise (my labour when I opened the door) for another (a smile or a thank you).

I know that this is only a small example, but it is merely to point out the subtle games of investment-for-return that we play. Many people live bitter and cynical lives because of this, they give, but remain mortally wounded when there is not a return. I don't want to labour the point, enough to say that when you give it will always return. Perhaps not directly, or even immediately. Often the return is not even from the person you have given to, but it will return.

Give, and make giving one of the reasons why you want to succeed. Help others, return the phone call when there is no obvious profit, write back to the person who you know has nothing to offer in return, go the extra mile for a complete stranger, and then tell no one of your good deed. Even the praise of others is not a profit when you go around saying, 'You'll never guess what I did today.' Make your charity anonymous. Seek neither praise nor recognition. Don't look for accolades for being a great guy (or gal). What a fantastic reason for wanting to get to the top, so you can help others to do the very same.

I must come clean here, too. I do not do half as much for others as I should and I too have fallen into all the traps;

expected a return, told others about my good deeds, been upset when I didn't get acknowledged, the lot, I've done it all wrong but every day I am practising to get it right. Only the big Girl in the sky gets ten out of ten all the time, but I will keep practising, and my intention is to succeed because a giving person who expects nothing in return is at the top of my 'would–aspire-to-be-like' list.

Someone recently asked me why I keep pushing myself, why I keep setting hard-to-get goals. And do you know the question really made me think hard? Why am I such a hard-taskmaster? Even as a child I was always trying to scale the highest trees (without the use of nails). Is it the money? I don't think so. I like money as much as the next guy, I like what it can bring me and my family, but there are many gigs I turn down because I have no love for them, despite the fact that they are extremely lucrative. So it can't be the cash (although it is not a bad goal in itself, as long as you do not allow money to become your god). When it came down to it I realised that my main reason, one of many but nevertheless the main one, was that I liked the feeling of winning. Not necessarily winning over or beating *others*, rather it was the feeling of beating myself.

Beating my last goal, the joy, the satisfaction, and the buzz of another success. The knowledge that each new goal I achieved served to expand my belief system and make the next goal more gettable. I loved the stretch, I loved the feeling of being overwhelmed, scared, knee-deep in the brown stuff, and then of overcoming all these obstacles to arrive at yet another winning post.

And I love – actually I am in love with – the fact that after each goal I reward myself (and my wife and family) with treats. The treat is normally proportionate to the goal. My last goal (shared jointly by Sharon and I) was to successfully complete a 32-city book tour, promoting *Watch My Back*, aiming to visit about 50 to 60 bookshops. This was all in a 6 to 8 week period. It was a mammoth task that stretched me further than any tour had before. I had planned the tour in my bid to get *Watch My Back* into the bestsellers list (anything in the top 5,000 is considered a bestseller – there are around one million other titles to compete with). We managed a delightful and hugely successful No. 21 in the *Sunday Times* biography bestsellers list. Our reward? We are here now, on a Caribbean cruise.

My rewards have varied from as little as an afternoon tea at a great café in town to a Rolex watch or even a new car. Often it is the little incentives that pull you through when everything else is pulling you down. On the last tour (we thoroughly enjoyed it by the way, despite the punishing schedule. We loved visiting all the bookshops, meeting the wonderful booksellers and our friends), I would frequently say to Shaz (or her to me) when times were hard, 'Don't worry, we'll be in the Caribbean before you know it.' And by gawd, here we are.

My son was recently recruited to sing in the choir at church. Now for some reason he got it into his head that this was going to be a terrifying ordeal. I tried everything I knew to convince him that all would be well and that actually singing in the choir was not as life-threatening as it might first appear. I talked to him about fear, about how facing your fear is a strong and admirable thing to do. I even told him how great he would feel afterwards, and that it wasn't as though he had to sing solo (now that could be a nappy-filling ordeal when you're eleven years old, or forty years old come to think of it). But still it wasn't happening; he wasn't having any of it. He was genuinely scared to the point of tears. The problem was – I surmised – he had no reason, no incentive to get up there and exercise his tonsils in front of a bunch of church-going strangers. So I gave him a reason. 'Listen,' I said, 'I've got a course on tomorrow (a martial arts course) and we're going to be selling books and videos. I'll tell you what, you do the choir tonight, sing your little heart out and I'll let you help us sell the books and videos tomorrow, and the first sale you make, you keep.' He stopped crying. 'So what do you say, is it a deal?'

Suddenly, incentive injected, he had a good reason to keep his date with the choir, one that was of profit to him, and the next day he made £15 when he sold a video. I have to say that it didn't help his singing much, but it did help him to overcome his fears and reach his goal.

Recognition can also be a great reason, an incentive to get you out of the bed when the rain is falling and the cold has brass monkeys investing in fur marble-bags. To be recognised is one of the most basic human needs. People of all shapes and sizes, colours and creeds will often do more for recognition than they will for material rewards. This is one of the reasons why successful companies, especially those involved in any kind of sales, take great efforts to give recognition for any accomplishment, large or small. They know that in a highly-populated, hugely-competitive world such as ours, people need this kind of incentive to make them feel as though they matter and that their employers care. It's like a validation of their worth. We should never underestimate the power of this need. We should reward others. We should also recognise the need in ourselves. When energy is lacking and when enthusiasm is sparse, motivation is all.

Your reason may be even more basic than this. It may be simply the fact that you are tired to the bone of just scraping the mortgage each month. Your incentive may be the fact that you want to prove to your detractors that you are a winner, that you can be better than they think you are. Success, they say, is the sweetest revenge.

I have lost count of the number of people who told me I couldn't make it as a professional writer, who thought me pretentious for trying to be more than (they thought) I was. Did I let them hold me back, did I let them sap my reserve? On the contrary, I used these people for raw fuel, a massive incentive not to fail where and when they said I would. I made a mental list of their barbed comments and their sardonic and patronising smirks, refined this negative energy and turned it into turbo-drive. 'You think I can't do it?' I'd say to myself. 'Watch this space.' Interestingly, the ones that said I'd never make it (now that I have) tell everyone how they sat next to me at school.

When Summersdale first published me, one of the chaps I worked the doors with actually came up to me and said, 'I don't know if anyone's told you Geoff, but your book won't ever do any good outside of Coventry. Oh it may do OK locally, but it won't work anywhere else. I thought I should tell you.'

Well thank you very much (you patronising git), I'll know who to call if I'm ever looking for a PR man! (Not!)

Needless to say, this guy went on my list and I used his energy big time. So thank you, you know who you are.

For your information he's still working the doors and still talking the talk. Don't ever knock people like this, on the contrary, welcome them, use what they give you. People of this ilk are a great incentive, great fuel on the journey from where you are to where you want to be.

To conclude: make sure you have a good reason for wanting your goal. Make them strong, moral, and if possible multiple. Oh, by the way, be happy on the journey. There is a great power in happiness.

Phew! I need a break, it's 7.00 p.m., see you in the morning on the deck at Lido's café. The coffee's on me.

– Secret Five –

The Power of Happiness

5 a.m. Sailing towards Barbados – 8 January 2001
Be happy with what you have while pursuing what you want. Happiness is not a destination; the man who says he is going to be happy when he reaches so-and-so, or when he becomes such-and-such, probably never finds it. It's not on the map you see, happiness. It's not a tangible location that you can pay a taxi driver to take you to; rather it's a state of mind that anyone can learn to adopt.

We have been propelled into nirvana, but even nirvana, with all its white sandy beaches, beach-bars and bikini-clad beauties, is not happiness. If you are not happy now, where you are, with whom you are, and with what you have, the fact that you are arriving at one of the most beautiful locations on planet earth will not make a lot of difference. In fact I'm fibbing, it will make a difference, it'll probably make you even more sad because when you get there the happiness flower still will not blossom. Do you know when the suicide rate shoots through the ceiling? Christmas. The birthday of our Lord Jesus Christ. People become twice as unhappy at the exact time when others think they should be hitting-the-ceiling high. It is this exact expectation that makes many people gloomy. They're sat there amidst the holly and the ivy ('When they are both full grown,' join in the chorus if you know the words) and thinking, 'Why aren't I bursting-at-the-seams happy?' The fact that they don't feel overjoyed makes them sad, and the sadness makes them perpetually unhappy to the point where people say, 'What's up with you? You look dead miserable. It's Christmas for flip's sake, cheer up.' Have a wild guess at the reaction to a comment like this. It sends a depressive personality on a downward spiral that can take weeks to recover from. Sometimes they never recover. Happiness is not a destination, so you have my permission to stop looking for it. And stop being sad or disappointed if you reach your Barbados and the internal fireworks refuse to respond to the touch-paper. Neither is happiness a time of year or a special person or a dream house or a loads-of-money bank account. These babies can weigh you down and cause you more sadness if you expect any more from them than material satisfaction.

I have a couple of elderly friends who live life for the lottery; before that they lived for the football pools. Why? Because if they won either, happiness (they believe) would be in abundance. They'd move house, they'd get a bigger car and they'd not have to worry about the bills. All the stuff that makes lottery-types pay handsome amounts to be in with a one-in-an-umpteen-million chance of winning. You know, I dread the day should they ever win a large amount of money. I dread it because they'd be extremely disappointed when they realised that happiness is not a destination. I absolutely dread them winning because their dreams would shatter like a dropped crystal. Can you imagine being handed enough cash to furnish all of your materialistic desires, only to realise that happiness still eludes you? Happiness is a state of mind, it's not an amount of money, it's not a locale or a new house.

I'm not saying that money doesn't lighten the load; of course it does. I'm not saying there isn't a high when you get a big deal; or that when the cash is shoved through your letterbox, that there isn't a nice buzz; there is, it can be lovely, but honestly it's more about running the race than it is about receiving the ribbon.

I was always scared as a youth. Well, I say I was always scared, that's not strictly true, it started for me from about the age of 11, when I went from primary school to comprehensive – 'big school'. After being the top kid at junior school, I found my new minnow status – just one of hundreds from all the schools in the area – overwhelming. It caused me lots of unhappiness and as a consequence I allowed myself to become the victim of bullies. I'm not blaming them. On the contrary, the problem was mine not theirs, I was too sensitive and I allowed others to intimidate me. The point of this story is that I decided to become a black belt in karate so that I could stand up for myself (and here's where I went wrong) and get rid of the feeling of fear. I was living with the belief that if I arrived at black belt – my nirvana, my Barbados – I would no longer feel fear. I'd seen black belts and presumed by their confident gait that they were fearless. That's where I wanted to be. Now wanting to be a black belt is a laudable goal, wanting to be money-rich is a great goal also. Both of these goals are fine destinations, as long as you don't expect too much from them. Both, when acquired, will bring major benefits, that's for sure, but neither will bring you happiness if you don't already have it.

I wanted to be a black belt to get rid of the fear. I knew that when the fear was gone I would be happy. When I did get my black belt many years later, there was the initial high that always comes with attaining a hard and long-term goal, but then came the massive depression, when I suddenly realised that I still felt fear. It hadn't gone, in fact, I now felt more fear than before. The game had, in my mind, suddenly got bigger and subsequently the stakes were higher. I was a black belt now; people expected so much more of me than before. They absolutely demanded that I be a fearless warrior with chilled blood and hands that needed to be licensed with the police. I felt no such thing. The worst part was, I now expected so much more of myself and when it was not forthcoming I fell apart like a cheap suit. I can't tell you how low I felt.

My mistake, as I said, was expecting fear to go away, I thought I'd be fearless. I expected my destination to bring happiness. Of course I now realise that this is folly, fear is a fundamental, biological must-have. We can't get rid of it, neither should we want to, fear is a survival mechanism without which the species would follow the dodo (as in 'dead as').

Fear, if employed properly and mastered, is a fantastic fuel that can be transmitted and used in any direction. My prolific workload today has not come about *in spite* of my fear, it is *because* of it. I am where I am because I experience loads of fear, but I have learned to cope with its power and use it to attain my goals. I did this by confronting the things that frightened me most and learning to control the flow, but more importantly I stopped trying to get rid of it. I started to expect and welcome it, especially when facing new challenges. All I did was alter my perception of fear because I realised that happiness did not come from ridding myself of it, rather it came from accepting adrenalin as a natural and necessary biological survival mechanism. In short, I changed my perception and fear became my ally. This whole story is in *Watch My Back* and details of overcoming and using fear are in *Fear – the Friend of Exceptional People* and if you are really stressed out then take a gander at *A Book for the Seriously Stressed* (formerly *Small Wars*).

So change your perspective, change your state of mind, in fact, if it is not serving you then change your whole mind. I'd recommend you read any book about Mahatma Gandhi, because this incredible man spent his whole life doing just that, changing his mindset. In fact, I'd recommend that you form a habit of reading anything and everything you can get hold of about self-improvement. Make a habit of reading inspirational books about (or by) great men and women, the high achievers of the world. There is a wealth of information out there that will, I assure you, change who you are. I am not suggesting that it's just a matter of reading a book and expecting it all to happen, of course not, but the right book is the trigger that can help break the inertia.

Influences

I'm on this huge ship now (the sun has just come up and it is another beautiful morning) and we have been sailing for two days, from Aruba to Barbados. But the ship would not be able to move very far unless someone switches on the engines. Someone has to act (and 'act' is the pivotal word here, one action is worth a ream of words). For me, reading the right book is my equivalent to switching on the engine. Looking back, I have been at my most prolific whilst inspired by a book. Books are brilliant, readers are leaders, and small libraries make great men and women.

I have some hugely successful friends who all attribute at least part of their wealth and success to at least one particular book. It is such a powerful medium. Of course, you can now get most books on audio, so you can listen in the car or on any long journey where perhaps reading is not appropriate (it's hard to read while you drive, I find that I keep spilling my coffee). Imagine how many hours a year you spend in the car. If you are in the car for even one hour a day, that's a total of 365 hours in a year. 365 hours! That's incredible. So if you listen to a motivational or learning tape, just whilst in the car, you're getting 365 hours of instruction and motivation a year. That's an incredible amount of learning, a fabulous investment in the most important person in the world. You! You may think you're not the most important person, you may say (or think) that it's your wife or your children, your mum or your dad, but it's not. It's you. If the captain is not in good shape the crew will be affected. If you're not alright how can you make it right for those around and connected to you?

So happiness is a state of mind that is affected profoundly by what it ingests and what it is influenced by: books, records, environment, who you speak with, listen to, live with, what you watch on TV, the sounds coming from your radio and of course, how you speak to yourself, your own internal dialogue.

Fortunately, we have the power to choose all these things. And believe me, you are a product of what surrounds you. It affects who you are, in fact it moulds who you are. If you think these things do not affect you, think again. Companies spend millions on advertisements so that they can influence, even change your mind, so that you favour their products. And it works; they don't spend that kind of money for nothing. Did you ever watch a horror movie as a kid (or even as an adult) and were affected so much that you couldn't sleep at night? When *The Exorcist* was first released it affected people, some so badly that they went mad, it created a psychosis – some even killed themselves. Conversely, many people were changed forever and for the better when they watched a depiction of the life of Jesus Christ, or Mahatma Gandhi. One of my friends was recently awed to the point of conversion after watching a film about the Dalai Lama. We have the power to change the films we watch if they are not influencing us in a way we would choose. My daughter wanted to watch *The Exorcist* at the cinema. 'What do you think dad, should I go and see it?' she asked.

'Well,' I replied, 'do you want to pay good money to be scared to the point of not sleeping? That's the question you should be asking yourself.' Of course she didn't want that, actually she only wanted to go to see what the fuss was all about. She decided that 'the fuss' wasn't worth paying for; she went instead to watch an empowering movie. You choose, it's down to you.

The Dalai Lama believes – and I agree – that life is about being happy. Will filling your head full of negativity make you happy? If not, that's a good enough reason not to do it. You have the power to choose, that's the secret, that's the joy, that's why I love my life because I know that if it don't feel good, I can change it for the better and forever.

It all starts with you. It is not the fault of others. Change the man and the world will be alright. We are all products of our thoughts, so start by changing what you think about all day long. And the good thing is that we can also change what we think if our current mode of thought does not empower us. Thought is so powerful that it is both frightening and at the same time awe-inspiring. Frightening because we can think ourselves into illness, we can think ourselves depressed, we can even think ourselves useless. Many have, and their thoughts made it so. What we have to realise – and this has been proven in medical tests the world over – is that our body hears and responds to every thought we have. If we think the same negative thoughts often enough they will become our reality. I had a friend in the services who thought he had contracted the AIDS virus. At the time there was a lot of publicity about the spread of this killer disease and he convinced himself that he had it. He'd had a bit of a lingering cold and happened to read in a tabloid newspaper that this was one of the many symptoms. Thousands of people probably entertained the same notion at the time, I'm sure. He allowed a small seed, an assumption, to enter his consciousness and before he knew where he was it had spiralled out of control. The negative thoughts became worries, and the worries became depression. In the end he seemed to be a magnet for newspapers, magazines, TV reports and even conversations about AIDS. All of which, in his depressed, paranoid state of mind, seemed like omens or signs that he'd got the disease. Because of the worry he lost his appetite, and because of this he ate less (if at all) and subsequently lost weight. Losing weight was also one of the symptoms of AIDS (so he read) so this added to his worries. People noticed his weight loss and felt it was their duty to tell him, 'Hey, you've lost some weight.' This has a powerful effect. It is as though your friends and associates are confirming your thoughts. In a very short time my friend became ill. He didn't have AIDS, though he truly believed by now that he did, but he was ill. Malnutrition, depression and the perpetual worry had fed off his negative thoughts. He was heading for a nervous breakdown. In the end his mum, very concerned about his health, managed to get the truth out of him. She was a lovely and sympathetic lady. She convinced him that all of his symptoms were merely the product of an overactive imagination. It wasn't until he eventually visited his doctor and had a blood test that he was finally convinced that he wasn't dying. Once the blood tests came back clear his appetite returned, his phantom symptoms disappeared and his weight returned to normal. His only disease was a single negative thought; a seed that grew into a monstrous ball of life-sapping worry.

Once I recognised the power of even a single thought, self-planted or planted by outside influences, I developed a mental guard, an internal vigilance that kept negative thoughts at bay. If they did manage to sneak in I developed methods of getting them back out again. It's not enough to read this book. This will start the engine running, but you have to engage the clutch and bang your foot on the accelerator. You can be inspired to act by a book, but it is you that has to take the first step. But how do you control thought? Good question. I was just coming to that very subject.

– Secret Six –

The Power of Thought

6.15 a.m. Caribbean Sea – 9 January 2001

The sun is just rising and is lighting the ocean into an aqua blue. Another beautiful day. It doesn't get much better than this I have to tell you. There are only a handful of us on deck at the moment. The dawn was shared by the half-dozen (out of the 2,000 or so on board) who managed to get up in time to see the birth of a brand new day. The start of a new life. Gandhi said that every night he went to sleep and awoke the next morning into a brand new life. The start of a new incarnation. It certainly feels like that here today. I'm going to celebrate this birth with a very hot, very fresh decaffeinated coffee. Excuse me.

I'm back (was I gone long? I got talking to my friend Lynn, one of the lovely passengers on the cruise). I have to tell you that I am surrounded by the most outstanding beauty, I love the ocean, especially at this time of the day. It's weird, I feel almost a part of it. It's a bit like Sharon and me; I'm not quite sure where she ends and I begin.

The Looking Glass Self

Have you ever been on the cusp of an exciting life change and then, right at the last moment allowed others to talk you out of it (or even scare you out of it)? Have you ever had a genius idea that could have revolutionized your life but that you later binned because your mates down the pub told you not to be stupid? Or perhaps you gave up on the possibility of a dream career because someone told you that you were not good enough? Do you find yourself sometimes aborting a great premise before it is even fully formed because that voice in your head says, 'Don't kid yourself, no one will take you seriously'?

You're not on your own. The majority of us (psychologists believe up to 95 per cent) have the same problem. We let our associates determine our destiny because we allow *their* words to become *our* thoughts.

Sociologists have a theory called 'The Looking Glass Self'. They say that we tend to become what our strongest influences believe we are. From my own experience I have found this to be frighteningly true. If our family, close friends and workmates believe that we are destined to sweep floors, then as likely as not – and before very long – we will find ourselves pushing a broom and thanking our lucky stars that we lived up to their expectations. A friend in prison once wrote to me to ask how I became a writer. I replied, 'My mum always said I could be a writer and I didn't let her down.'

He replied in his next letter, 'My dad always said I'd be a jailbird so I guess I didn't let him down either.'

Unfortunately our thoughts are not always our own as much as we'd like to think they are; they are intrinsically linked to those around us. Often we find ourselves surrounded by folk who see the world as unfair and unjust. People who fall into the blame trap and give over their power to some exterior force – not strong influences to be around because procrastination is a very infectious disease that can kill potential like a swatted bluebottle. They are metaphoric sandbags strapped to those of us who want to fly our balloons. Bearing this in mind, and if your intent is to do more with your life than lament over the morning coffee, you have to start by choosing your influences wisely.

Our minds are often built (or burnt) by our external influences. Success in any shape or form will always be back-breakingly difficult if your influences are not empowering. If they are constantly pulling you down then as likely as not, unless you change them in a hurry, down is exactly where you are going to slide. This is something that most of us (secretly) know, so no surprises there. What may surprise you is the fact that your greatest influence is not, as you may previously have thought, an external one. It's not your mum or your wife or your brother or your boss. It's not your environment. Your shit-trap is not the result of poor potty-training as a blarting nipper, neither is it a consequence of a vengeful God. Your life is not determined (unless you let it be) by what they say or what people around you think or even by what they do. Your greatest influence is someone a lot closer to home, someone you sleep with on a regular basis, the person that you share the shower with, the one that knows you better than anyone else. It is entirely possible that you don't even like this person (he knows too much about you). You can't hide from him, even when you close your eyes. (Have you guessed it yet?) It's you. You are your greatest influence. You're with yourself 24 hours a day, 7 days a week, and 365 days a year. You are stuck with yourself for a whole incarnation (about the same amount of time you get stuck with your ex-wife), so if you want to change your world you have to start by changing yourself.

Self-change

Self-change is fundamentally about altering the way you talk to yourself, your internal dialogue or what psychologists call sub-vocalisation. You have to alter your whole relationship with the only person in the cosmos that can really influence permanent and lasting change in your life. You. This is vital because if you don't you will sabotage and destroy any and every chance you have of making your life a success.

'Why,' I hear you cry, 'would we sabotage ourselves?'

It's simple. It's what we've been taught to do. Let me explain.

Any psychologist worth his PhD will tell you that we are a product of many things, not least our genes. We can't change our genes but we can work with them. I was born with a nervous disposition (my mum is fond of saying that I 'inherited her nerves'), an impediment for many but not for me – once I ultimately came to terms with it. I have learned to channel the hereditary energy excess that once triggered long, dark depressions into a prolific work ethic that has enriched my life in many ways.

Our environment plays a big part also; simply relocating to a locale that doesn't suck the life out of us can change the negative to positive. Whilst all these factors play a major role in forming the man you see in the shaving mirror every morning, the thing that possibly has the greatest impact on who we become is our upbringing. Certainly the way we talk to ourselves in the present can be directly attributed to how we were talked to in the past.

Freud believed that each of us, from around the age of five, develops an internal parent (what he called the super ego) which is moulded by our immediate influences; parents (especially), brothers and sisters, relatives, friends, trends, the environment and our culture. The super ego is the voice (sometimes voices!) in your head that guides your behaviour and tries to keep your morals and ethics in order. The problem is that whilst for most of us our biological parents brought us up to the best of their abilities, their information was – almost definitely not by intent – limited (hope me mum's not reading this). Their limitations become our limits, how they spoke to us as children is how we speak to ourselves as adults. Subsequently, by the age of 18, the average person has been told 'no' or 'you can't do it' 148,000 times. It's little wonder then that, as full-grown men or women 'with a mind of our own' our internal parent is still doing the job it was programmed to do (telling us 'no') and, as a consequence, 90 per cent of our internal dialogue is negative.

Our thoughts create *our* world! If our thoughts are negative and limiting, our world becomes the mirror image.

I told you the story of the elephant and the twig, about how, in India, they train obedience in young elephants (to stop them from escaping) by tying them to a huge immovable object, whereby they develop learned helplessness. Similarly with us humans; if we are told enough times that we cannot escape mediocrity, or that we cannot achieve our dreams, eventually that belief will become so strong, so real, that like the elephant, we'll believe it; it will become our truth. An immovable object that binds us to our lot. In the end no one has to tell us our place; we've heard it so often we start to tell ourselves. Hence, when we set our sights on the dream girl or the to-die-for job, our inner voice – well trained in the art of limitation – sets to work. Does it point out our strengths and look at our capabilities? No, it shuns the can-dos and rolls out the can'ts like a carpet of broken glass. Before we know it there are so many daunting and insurmountable obstacles in our own path that we abort the journey of a thousand miles without even taking the first step.

I had a friend, Jonnie, who was a great singer, everyone agreed he was fantastic. His dream was to make it in the music industry and he seemed destined to do just that. One evening when he was singing at a local venue a big talent scout spotted him. He told Jonnie that he had a lot of potential and wanted him to come to his offices in Manchester to sign a recording deal. Jonnie didn't even need to check the guy out, his reputation in the industry was legendary. All he had to do was make a trip to Manchester to dot the i's and cross the t's . It was a fantastic opportunity but Jonnie never took it because, all of a sudden, faced with success on a massive scale, he got scared. What if he got to the Manchester recording studio and they laughed him out of the building? What if he couldn't hack the pressure? What about his girlfriend, what would happen to her when he was off on tour? What about his life? All of a sudden, his dream manifesting before his very eyes, he started to feel trapped by success even though he hadn't even signed a contract. 'I won't even be able to go to the shops anymore without being hassled,' he told his mum. He never made the journey to Manchester and he never returned any of the phone calls from the talent scout. Subsequently he never made it into the higher echelons of the music world. Jonnie can still be seen playing his music at local venues. His own mind had defeated him before he'd even entered the music arena.

This story may be familiar to many, though perhaps your opponent was not the debilitating fear of signing a recording contract. Perhaps your incapacitating adversary was a big business deal, the decision to change jobs, go self-employed, move home, end a relationship or start a new one, ask the boss for a rise, travel the world, start up a new business, expand an existing business or whatever.

Do you think that I wasn't scared half to death when I had to travel to London to choreograph the fight scenes in a West End play? Of course I was. When I was first asked to do the play it was a tiny speck on the horizon, it wasn't even fully written when the author, Jim Cartwright, offered me the job. It was way off in the distance, it looked so small. I thought, 'Yeah, I can do that, no trouble.' The problem is that distant objects have a habit of getting bigger as they get closer. This one was no exception; it got bigger and bigger and bigger. In the end it got so close and so big that it blocked out everything else in my life until it was all I could see – and it was scary.

That's when I started thinking, 'This is a lot bigger than I thought it was. I don't know if I can deal with it any more.'

In reality the distant speck is no different to the horror that bashes on your front door. It's the same thing, just up closer. If you stand back and give yourself a bit of perspective it's not so big after all. And that's what happened with me and the West End play. As it got closer it got huge. What was once a project on paper suddenly became frighteningly real. I was asked to go to London every week to start training the actors, and I had to start writing out the fight sequences (one of the fights in the play lasted for over twenty minutes). I made the first trip and met the other people working on the play; designers, producers, directors and actors (one of the actors, Richard Hope, had won an Oscar, and another, Nick Woodeson, had been in Hollywood films). Every one of them was 'award winning this' or 'award winning that': even the guy sweeping the floors had won an award for 'the best kept broom'! They were all world-class and at the top of their trades. Me? I couldn't even spell choreography. Suddenly it was all too much for me. I was so close to this thing that it frightened me. I couldn't seem to find a way past my fear of going down to London and being absolutely useless. I thought to myself, 'I can't deal with this, it's massive.' But it wasn't massive, only in my own mind; I'd allowed it to overpower me. It is hard for the eyes to see what the mind has got completely out of focus. So I stood back from it to get a more realistic perspective. I changed my internal dialogue and said to myself, 'I *can* handle this. It might be the West End and these people might be top tradesmen but in my own field so am I. And anyway,' I added, 'all they want from me is realistic fight sequences. I have spent the last 30 years doing 'real' – in the martial arts clubs and on the doors – and if there's one thing I know it's what a real fight looks like.' I might have been incapable of spelling 'choreography' but I certainly did know my onions. I knew I could do this and do it well. And I wasn't the only one with trembling patellas. We were all a little nervous, it is only natural. It's when you let your nerves sprout roots that they grow out of proportion. I made my move, and not only worked on the play (six months in all) but I also picked up some great reviews in the broadsheets when the play finally came on at the Royal Court Theatre in London.

But of course it's not just what you say to yourself that does the damage, it is also what you listen to when others have their say.

The late Sir Stanley Matthews had his early notions of becoming a professional footballer kicked in the shins by the local newspapers. After watching Matthews in one of his early matches they said he'd never be more than a good local player. He proved them wrong by eventually making it to the England squad. But even then, after a bad performance against a strong German team, the national newspapers said that Matthews would never make it on the international circuit. Can you imagine reading that in the tabloids? The national newspapers saying that you haven't got what it takes? That kind of advice is enough to end any career. But did Matthews listen to the papers and allow negative thoughts to infiltrate his mind? Did he allow their thoughts and opinions to become his own? No, because he knew what he had, he knew he was good, he believed in himself and that's what he kept telling himself. Mr Matthews kept his internal dialogue positive and went on to become probably the best-known football player in the history of the game. He became a football genius and legend.

What we need to remember is that not everything we hear is true. Just because someone says you haven't got it doesn't make it so. J.K. Rowling of Harry Potter fame was inundated with rejection slips when she first sent her young wizard to the publishing houses of London. They felt her work unworthy of publication. If she had listened to them and allowed her inner dialogue to turn to rat's shit, the world would have been deprived of one of the most successful series of children's books in history (and she would have been deprived of the millionaire status, and great satisfaction, which followed the success of her work).

So I would advise you to change your environment if it is dragging you down, urge you to change your influences if they are pulling you back. Change your house, your job, and your friends if a spring clean is in order because all of these things affect the way you feel about yourself. Hell, if you think it will help, you can even change your hairstyle; but none of this will change your life if you don't start by changing yourself, or more specifically changing the way you talk to yourself.

Everything starts with a thought (and that's the secret). So 'thought' is where you have to start. Monitor and be very fussy about the thoughts you entertain. Train your mind not to think negative thoughts. How do you do this? The concept is simple (though the practice can be difficult) – don't think them. When they come into your mind, ignore them. Don't just sit there like a victim. When we focus on a thought we feed it, we fatten it and, like a watermelon seed, that thought grows to 350,000 times its own size. We often feel as though we have no control over our thoughts and that they came into our subconscious, uninvited, to rape and pillage. Let me tell you; the opposite is true. If there is one thing in this world we can control, it is our thoughts. They are just like wild horses that need breaking and training. This takes constant practice, daily (even hourly) attention until the mind that runs wild can be tamed and the massive energy channelled so that it serves us. An untrained mind, like a wild tiger, is unpredictable and dangerous.

This is one of the things that I find hugely exciting about life and about this wonderful kit that each of us is issued with (our bodies). We have a vehicle that has the potential, when trained, to give us all we could ever dream of having.

So getting the internal dialogue right is the first, the most important and, of course, the hardest step. Our thoughts are the very foundation upon which everything else is based. What we say and what we do are also vital, but our thoughts and actions find their roots in what we think. So once we get the thoughts right, the rest kind of follows.

So how can we practise thought?

Prayer

Prayer is one way of exercising the internal dialogue, or sub-vocalisation. You may or may not follow a set religion. If you do (or do not), no matter, prayer in reality is just one way of giving the internal dialogue a workout. I do pray every day but I am spiritual rather than religious. It's great training. You don't have to go to church to do this; every man is his own church. You can do it at the bus stop, in the bath, before you go to bed at night or in a traffic jam. I go for a walk most mornings, I do my praying then. Pray to God, pray to Buddha, pray to the cow in the farmer's field, you can pray to Blod (made-up name) or you can even pray to a tree (ancient Indians used to ask trees for answers to their questions). Put any name you want to it, no matter. The beauty that moves the cosmos, the presence that you will find when you split a log and lift a stone, will know whom you mean. Mother Theresa, a devout Catholic and saviour to thousands would often lead prayer practice to the masses in Calcutta. Many people from different backgrounds and beliefs would turn up to pray. She would use prayers from the Catholic faith, but always stipulated, 'When we get to the part in the prayer where I say Jesus Christ, feel free to replace it with any name you want.' (Or words to that effect). When I pray I try to make the basis of my prayer one of thanks and appreciation. It's important to be thankful.

Contemplation

The Dalai Lama recommends contemplation as a means of exercising positive and informative internal dialogue. This is another great way to exercise silent speak, to whittle your thoughts like an archer whittles down his wood to make an arrow. I practise contemplation; it's quite demanding, but very effective. Pick a subject (any subject) and spend 15 minutes, half an hour, an hour, whatever you can manage and contemplate its purpose. For instance, you might want to contemplate on a subject that, perhaps, you are struggling with. Wealth, forgiveness, jealousy, fidelity, infidelity, goals, charity, love, hate, anything. Choose a subject and debate it back and forward in your own mind. For instance, if you were contemplating wealth it may go back and forward something like this (I am just going to make this up as I go):

Wealth

Is wealth a good thing?

Yes, I'd say so.

What is wealth?

Well it can be an abundance of anything, money, love, charm, charisma; wealth means abundance.

What if you had an abundance of hate, would that still be wealth?

It depends upon your perspective. Hate is seen as a negative emotion – and of course it is – but if your perspective was positive you might look on that abundance as grist for the mill, a means to practise the art of forgiveness. Hate is a powerful emotion, emotion is a fuel and if directed properly that fuel could be used to energise your journey to somewhere positive.

Can wealth be bad?

Yes, if it is misused.

How can something you said is good be bad?

Wealth is a form of power, power can be used for good or for bad. Often power can corrupt people and they use it for bad reasons.

And what constitutes 'bad'?

I suppose bad can be anything that intentionally hurts others.

What if you are hurting someone for his or her own good, is that still bad?

I would say that it is only construed as bad when your intention is bad.

So if your intention is good that's OK?

I'd say so.

What if your intention was good but your information was wrong?

You can only act on the information that you have at any given moment. The main thing is that you believe your truth, and that your intention is for good and not for bad.

You can see where I'm going here (I hope), it's a mind debate that stretches your internal dialogue and it also stretches your knowledge. I have debated some very difficult subjects and come up with things that I had never thought of before – and at the same time practised my internal speech, or thought. You will come up with some very surprising and spontaneous questions and answers. That was just a short example of course, it can go back and forward for a very long time. Sub-vocally, it is prime workout. Though, as I said, it can be quite demanding.

Reading

When you read, you implant the thoughts or words of the writer into your own mind. Whilst you read, these thoughts become your thoughts, even if only temporarily. So, with this in mind stick to empowering, educational, motivational works. Reading is another great way to focus your thoughts and give them a long-distance run. I read a lot; I even took a speed-reading course, so that I could take in more. It takes a lot of mental discipline to read consistently but the benefits are huge.

Abstinence

This is an internal workout for giants. Buddhists practise it, some of the old-time boxers were keen advocates and my own hero Mahatma Gandhi built his whole world on a platform of abstinence.

Abstinence is the art of abstaining from certain thoughts, certain deeds, certain foods; it's the art of abstaining from anything really, though in my practice I only abstain from negatives, i.e. the things I think are bad for me.

I abstain from negative thinking, gossip, judging others, and alcohol. There is a continuing list of things that I abstain from, and I keep adding things all the time. It is believed that all our power is locked into our addictions and that when we kill them our power returns. In this society the global addictions are junk food, alcohol, drugs and pornography. All our power is locked in one, or all, of these. When we can kill them (abstain from them) we will be empowered.

You may see no relationship between these addictions and your happiness and success, you may not even think they are addictions. But if you try to give them up, even for one month, and you can't, then the chances are that they are addictions. The connection is very real. It affects you on a physical, mental and subsequently a spiritual level. It doesn't mean that if you have addictions that you can never be happy or successful. You can; some are, have been and will be in the future, but the happiness is never complete and the success is often at the expense of one's health. Your addiction also makes you vulnerable. You are – as they say – only as strong as your weakest link. Many of the great men and women of our species have been brought down from global heights purely by their weaknesses. You only have to look at the newspapers for proof of that. Pop stars lose their whole career (often their lives) because of their drink and drug addictions; in recent years were the tragic deaths of Michael Hutchence and the lovely Paula Yates to name but two. Gary Glitter, the disgraced pop star, recently lost a wonderful life because his weak link – paedophilia – was found out and his perversions exposed to the whole world. Even Bill Clinton, until recently one of the most powerful men in the free world, fell from grace when he was exposed as a liar and a cheat on national television over his extramarital affairs. Businessmen and women worth millions (even billions) die on a daily basis because of their addictions to work, junk food, drugs or pornography (or a combination of all).

By courting addictions you clog your vehicle, so it is never quite working on full throttle. The chemicals we ingest when we take in rubbish (food or information) affects us on every level. Also the chemicals we produce (or should I say over-produce) when indulging in junk food, drink, drugs and hard pornography have a terrible effect on our physical and mental well-being. Popular magazines endorse the belief that pornography is OK. Some even recommend it as a spice to good sex. Morally you have to make your own mind up. I'm not here to preach or offend or even to tilt a lance. Physically and mentally though, hardcore pornography can be both addictive (once you pop you can't stop) and unhealthy. The amount of stress hormones released when exposed to hard and often abusive porn is harmful to your entire well-being. Paradoxically, if you do have an addiction to booze, drugs, hardcore porn or junk food (or any unhealthy addiction), they can be great training tools to develop massive internal control if you can overcome and abstain from them. This is just a suggestion, you may want to give it a look or you may want to give it the elbow. It is your choice.

Now last time I wrote about this people were offended. Some said, 'Love the philosophy, but I'm not giving up the booze/drugs/porn, etc.' Let me reiterate: I am not saying any of these things are right or wrong. I am not judging. I have a biblical plank in my eye that will not allow me to judge others. All I'm saying is, 'It's great training if you do manage to give up.' You want to build an indomitable spirit, you want to develop a sinewy mentality? There is no better way than abstinence. It's not the only way, there are other routes to the top of the mountain, but this is one of the best, it is certainly fast-track stuff. If it doesn't work for you that's OK too, but check it out. Have a think about it, contemplate its benefits. You may feel that you could never do without a beer (I did), but believe me, once you let the addictions go you feel empowered. And it's not as if I sit here of an evening thinking, 'My life's terrible because I can't have a beer.' On the contrary, I don't miss it at all, and my life is so much better because I have kicked my addictions into touch. I happened to mention to a friend that I was practising abstinence and that I had given up alcohol. Well, I thought he was going to fall over he was so shocked. 'I'm not doing that,' he complained, even though I never suggested he should. 'What's the point of it all if I can't even have a beer of a night?' He was defensive and upset at even the mention of the idea.

If your life is so drab that there is no point in it all (as my friend said) if you can't have a beer then (Houston) we have a problem. Reactions such as this are not a good sign. As I tried to explain to my friend, I am not judging, how could I with my varied and colourful background? And neither would I wish to, I am merely offering objective information that can help you on your journey. Hate it or heed it, you choose, just don't shoot the messenger. It is simply a truth that I have learned and would like to pass on to those with an interest. I am too busy working on my own addictions to be worried (or judgmental) about yours.

All this falls nicely into one category: discipline. So anything that demands a locus of internal control is good practice. Physical training is another great method of discipline. It is also a great way of expelling surplus and caustic stress chemicals from your body. It certainly gives you a mental workout, because just getting to the gym on a hot day, a cold morning or a rainy evening takes loads of self-control and self-motivation.

Like most things of worth, you get what you work for, but if you stop working you stop getting. What you don't use you lose. So when you take on these new disciplines, take them on for life if you want the fruits for life. You can abstain from certain things temporarily if you like, but the benefits tend only to last as long as you abstain. If you go back to your old ways, you drop back to your old standards. Hard truth I know, but truth nonetheless. On the plus side, if you pick the workload back up again after a lay-off, your body and mind remembers its past peaks and will get you back on-line again quite quickly.

It's 6.15 p.m. and a coffee on deck watching Sharon do a step class is calling – see you early, if you can make it.

5 a.m. Somewhere in the Caribbean Sea.

Have you noticed how simple it is to fall into negative speech patterns and how easy it is for others to implant negative thoughts into your mind? Most of what is spoken from one person to another, even amongst strangers, is negative. You're at a bus stop, walking in the park, waiting at the dentist's surgery when someone says, 'Nasty weather.' You find yourself repeating, as expected, 'Yes, I know, isn't it awful?' You say this even though you perhaps do not truly agree. Personally, I love the rain. As a species we are made up of something like 95 per cent water, so my thinking when the rain falls is, 'These are my brothers and sisters.' Water is life-affirming. I take regular walks around Coombe Abbey, a local country park in Coventry, England. I love all the seasons, but the rainy season is one of my favourites. There is no better feeling than wrapping up in a warm hat and coat, and walking in the rain. I love the feeling of it dashing into my face. It's invigorating and if you ever get to go to somewhere like Florida, USA, you'll get to see proper rain (or as Forrest Gump might say, 'big old fat rain') where it comes down in chunks the size of half-crowns (if you don't remember half-crowns, they're about the size of a small dinner plate).

So when I take my walk and I pass people, and they say to me, as they invariably do, 'Awful weather,' I reply, 'I love the rain.' I get a few funny looks, but it keeps me from being impregnated with anything negative. The rain is good, the snow is pretty, the wind is dead relaxing, and ice? Any excuse to get the tea tray out and slide down hills. There is no bad weather unless you make it so. It may sound as though I'm talking semantics here, you may even think that I am being idealistic (which I am and proud of it), but really the weather is just the start. 'It's a terrible day,' is just a few short steps from, 'It's a terrible week, I've had a shit year, my life is awful, isn't the world a bad job?' Get into the habit of affirming the positive. When someone says, 'How are you?' don't say, 'Not bad,' because 'not bad' means 'not good either'. How do you want your day to be? I want mine to be fantastic. So when someone says, 'How are you?' Say, 'Fantastic actually, what a kicking life.' When they say, 'How's your day?' say, 'Brilliant, every day is Christmas.' Don't talk yourself into a bad day, a bad week, a bad holiday or a bad life.

I can remember how me and Sharon — after a terrible flight over to America — talked ourselves into being bad flyers.

We took the kids to Florida one year and, for the first time ever, we had a bit of a bumpy flight (you know it's been a bad one when the passengers break into spontaneous applause as the plane lands at its destination). When we got off the plane Sharon said something flippant like, 'That was a bad flight.' And I think I replied, with equal flippancy, 'Yes, I know, I nearly filled my nappy.'

Over the space of the next two weeks we spoke many times about how bad the flight was, and how we hoped the flight back would be better. By the end of the two-week holiday we had engaged this negative mode of thinking to such an extent that we were actually dreading the flight home. As it turned out the flight was fine, but due to the fact that we had talked 'bad flight' for the whole holiday we felt every little bump and turn, and if we hit turbulence the adrenalin raced like a crazed greyhound rabbit. It didn't end here. It was a year until we went to America again, and in that time Sharon and I actually talked ourselves into being bad fliers by reminiscing about the bad flight that we had had (we were actually telling people in the end that we were bad fliers and that we hated aeroplanes). Then I got an offer to teach in America for Chuck Norris, a fantastic opportunity that I nearly declined because I didn't want to fly. And Sharon didn't want to fly either. Then I cottoned on to what had occurred, or more specifically, what I had allowed to occur. I had allowed one negative flight and one negative thought to grow so big that it became my reality. My thought had become actual. I quickly changed my mind by telling myself, and every one that I talked with, that I was a great flyer, that I loved aeroplanes and that I couldn't wait to fly again. As the America trip grew closer I told myself that we were going to have a great flight, the best ever, and that I was going to enjoy every moment of it. I never once allowed myself to think 'bad flight'. And it was fantastic; the trip was great and all because I made it so with my thoughts.

As I said, your body listens and responds to everything you say. If you want illness, just keep telling yourself over and over again that you are ill, and it will happen. If you think that the rain is depressing, guess what? Every time it rains you'll get what you ordered, melancholia. What we say, how we speak, what we think and our phraseology has long been linked with illness and disease. You talk yourself into colds or flu; you talk yourself into headaches and backaches. How many times have you heard someone say (or said yourself), 'Every time there is a cold going round, I get it'? And *voila*, every time there's a cold or flu in the air, you, by royal command, do actually get it. I have a pensioner friend who tells me whenever I meet her, 'Geoff, I am never well!' Don't say that! Not unless never being well is your wish. Your body listens to every word you say. If you don't want to succeed just tell yourself, 'I'll never get this, I'll never succeed,' and (lo and behold) you probably won't. There is no such thing as 'can't', but how many people invite disappointment into their lives and create a self-fulfilling prophecy by saying, 'I could never do that!' We are too fond of statements that nick the power right out of our bones like, 'I never was any good at that.' I had a couple of difficult times at school with mathematics. I didn't enjoy the class and I cemented my inability to juggle numbers by repeating over and over whenever the subject came up, 'I've never been good at maths.' Please don't say that, don't say it. You are what you think; if you think 'ill' you are signing a get-me-ill-and-in-a-hurry chit. If you think 'sad', 'unhappy', 'incapable', 'boring' or 'bad company' then you'll get just what you ordered. You created it.

It often starts when we are growing up and someone tells us, or tells company while we're in hearing distance (kids hear, even though you might think they don't), 'Oh, he's not academic, he's never been good at school', 'His brother is the bright one', 'He hasn't got a musical ear', 'He's terrible at sport', 'He's stupid'. Just the thought of all this negativity makes me cringe. How many times have you heard a parent tell a child they are a 'stupid boy/girl' or 'a very bad boy/girl'? When kids are young and their brains are forming, they are like a blank hard drive on a computer. Blank until you load them with instructions for life – and they do last for life.

I had a girlfriend who had a lovely body, but she walked around with her shoulders scrunched over and her beautiful breasts hidden. She actually walked with a stoop to hide her bust. It turned out that when she was young and just developing, her father made a cruel comment about the fact that one breast was slightly different in size than the other (which is the case for something like 95 per cent of all women). Actually, it was less of a comment and more of an attack; a cheap shot aimed at getting a laugh. He had a habit of crushing her with such statements when they had company. She'd just dressed for a night out with friends and the top she wore was figure hugging. 'You've got one boob bigger than the other,' he said, and then laughed. Twenty years later she still walked with a stoop.

It took me a long time to bring her confidence back and get her walking and standing straight. I did this by affirming and reaffirming that she was a beautiful lady and that she had a fantastic bust (it was a hard job, but someone had to do it).

The Past

A lot of our thoughts are in the past. This is not good because the past is dead, it is no more. So why reside there? That's what you do when you allow your thoughts to drift back. It is an investment with no positive return. Many of us revisit the past to dig up the bodies of our mistakes. We bring them back to life and re-run the scenarios when we were at our worst. We do it with a sense of regret in the spirit of 'if only'. They say you can't change the past, but you can kill it. Not too difficult when you consider that it's colder than a two-day-old lasagne anyway. If the future is our aim then we have no right to keep anchoring ourselves to the past. You are unlikely to move very far forward towards tomorrow or even enjoy the today, when you have one foot (or even your whole self) planted somewhere in the past. Let it go, kill it, don't even allow yourself one second of retrospect (other than to use the past as a positive reference point to solve a current problem). When you hear the statement 'living in the past' it's dead right. You can't be there and here at the same time. We often indulge ourselves in the past and revisit our old injustices. We entertain melancholy thoughts and tell ourselves about how hard we had it and how unjust people, circumstances, the environment, luck or God were to us.

We wallow in the self-pity of retrospect and talk about the fact that we can't get over it, or can't forgive those that did us harm intentionally or inadvertently. Get a life! Stop feeling sorry for yourself, stop being weak and let that baby go. Let it all go. They are not hurting you, *you* are hurting you. Do yourself a favour; forgive the past and sever those disabling ties, because it does you no service. See how you fly when you drop the sandbags from your balloon. Living in the past is an indulgence for the self-pitying and the weak. A very selfish act that hurts everything you touch in the present and that poisons every projection you have for the future.

It is said that you cannot change the past, but I think you can. When you kill it you change it. When you refuse it even a second thought, when you forgive your mistakes and you forgive others, the past no longer exists unless you allow it living space in your mind. It doesn't matter what they have done to you. If you don't forgive them, they are still doing it to you and it'll be your fault because you're letting it happen. If killing the past doesn't change it then I don't know what does. If people hurt you in the past, use the lesson to make sure it doesn't happen again in the future. If you hurt others, learn your lesson and don't make that mistake twice. I made lots of mistakes in the past, more than most people, but I don't carry them around with me. I don't need others to forgive me because I forgive myself. When you forgive yourself no one can punish you – even though they may want to – because you won't let them.

I have also been hurt many times in my life, but I am still here. So it couldn't have been all that bad. I thank those people that hurt me (honestly), I forgive them, each and every one, but most of all I thank them for their contribution to this bubbling piece of happiness that is me, sat at a table on deck looking into the ocean. If even one of my life events did not happen in the way it did – both good and bad – I would not be here, on my way to the island of Antigua having the time of my life. And I am not being a great bloke here when I talk about forgiveness. I'm not looking for a pat on the back or a medal or admiration or even sympathy. Certainly not. I wouldn't give you tuppence for any of that. I am forgiving others (all of them, no exceptions) because it is good for me. Forgiveness is a very selfish (but a good and empowering selfish) act. It helps me. That's why I do it.

Place a stop-check on the negative inner dialogue and start courting some positive, empowering parley. Talk to yourself with a lot of respect, with a bundle of love. Think about the person you love most in the world, the person that you would do anything for, the one that you are kindest to. Treat yourself like you treat that person. Treat yourself fantastically. It's not always easy, you may have to work on it every day until it becomes a habit. But it'll be a habit well worth courting. And don't allow others to talk to you like you're a piece of garbage. You're not, so don't have any of it.

The difficulty, of course, comes in implementing these essentials after a lifetime of being talked down to by others and yourself. Made habits have to be unmade. This will take gallons of daily practice and chunks of self-discipline. It will mean checking yourself and others and stopping negativity before it starts, and not allowing seeds of doom and doubt to impregnate your mind. This is the prerequisite to reprogramming yourself so that your thoughts lift and do not limit you; so that they shoot you to the stars instead of dragging you through the mud; so that they nourish and nurse your aspirations instead of hitting them on the head with a blunt instrument.

One final sentiment. I learnt it from living in my own past for a long time. Forgive the past, or stop moaning about the fact that your life stinks.

Your thoughts are your world, make them grand, and change them if they do not serve you, if you are struggling to get going, use some inspiration to give you energy. How do you get inspiration? Funny you should ask. What are you doing in the morning? Meet you on deck, early.

– Secret Seven –

The Power of Inspiration

6.15 a.m. Caribbean – 10 January 2001

Inspiration is the fuel that gets you to your destination. No fuel, no journey. If you wanted to go on a long journey in the car, what's the first thing you'd do? Probably you'd fill it up with fuel. The journey towards your goal or to success is no different. You need fuel and you need plenty of it. So I'd like to look at some of the ways we get the inspirational fuel to power our voyage.

Books

I've written about books before, about the power of books, about the secrets that lie between the pages. History is recorded in books and just about every successful person since time began has written down the secrets of success. So with a visit to the local bookshop or to the library you can open this treasure trove too. I have read, and continue to read, many. I consider it the very best investment I can make in myself. Besides the fact that books contain earth-moving information, they are also probably the best source of inspiration you can get. You can read about Messner, Gandhi, the Dalai Lama, the Pope, Richard Branson. You can read of great adventurers, presidents, kings and queens. You can read rags-to-riches or even riches-to-rags stories. You can read about men and women who changed the course of history almost – and sometimes entirely – single-handedly. You can read about how Columbus discovered the Americas, how

Mohammed Ali went from a village kid to Heavyweight Champion of the world or how Pélé, probably the greatest footballer in the history of the game, honed his skills kicking coconuts barefoot on a Brazilian beach (ouch!).

They laughed at Lowry you know!

What about Lowry? The renowned painter of matchstick men and matchstick cats and dogs (join in the chorus if you know the words.) How did this rent collector from Manchester, England go from local dabbler (in art) to global artist? How did he overcome his detractors? How did he develop his art? Why did he turn down a knighthood? You can read about how the Queen Mother moved him onto the world stage when she bought one of his works, how the influence of his mother (she never rated him as an artist) nearly ended his career and how he continued, despite ridicule. They laughed at Lowry you know. They did. And when I read that in his biography, when I read that people laughed and scoffed at this lovely and sensitive man, it was great solace to me because when I was up-and-coming, people laughed at me too. I remember an occasion when I got in touch with my mate to tell him some good news. I'd just won an international development award for my film script *Watch My Back* (based on my book by the same name) and I had to tell someone – it's what you do when providence lights your day. But when I told him, I didn't get the response I'd expected. Quite the opposite actually. 'Oh yeah,' he said half-scoffing, half-laughing. 'I suppose it'll be the Oscars next then?' His attitude landed like a heavy right. There was bitterness in his tone that made me regret the call.

'Well yeah,' I replied (a bit too defensively). 'If that's what I intend to do then why not? Why not? There's a guy in Preston, Nick Park, who's won four!' (If I have to I'll go and get one of his).

After putting down the receiver, still reeling from his unexpected response, I reminded myself (sub-vocally of course) that my friend's attitude need not slaughter my day, neither should I ever let him, or others, hold me back. Criticism, cynicism and jealousy are a familiar trinity, often encountered when leaving a muddy comfort-zone en route to a starry ideal. I wasn't the first to be laughed at for daring to dream, neither would I be the last.

When a young German climber told friends of his bold intentions to climb solo the perilous mountain Nanga Parbat – a feat never before attempted, let alone achieved – they didn't just laugh at him, they called him insane. Equally insane was the idea that two men – with an investment of only $30, a penchant for good ice cream and absolutely no experience – could one day take on confectionery giant Häagen Daz. Reinhold Messner climbed Nanga Parbat solo only six weeks after conquering Everest without oxygen and Ben and Jerry turned their $30 investment into a billion dollar giant-slaying industry. Who's laughing now?

And they laughed at Lowry too. When he first put his brush to canvas the haughty elite of contemporary art held their chuckling bellies and laughed the gentle northerner out of Manchester. They slurred him at every opportunity for trying to be more than (they thought) he was. They called this lovely working-class rent collector, working out of Pall Mall, an amateur and his work (at best) naïve. 'Who does he think he is?' they asked. Later, when the sugar pedestals of the (so-called) mighty had crumbled under the strength and beauty of Lowry's vision and his genius shone through the oils, Lowry had the last laugh – bidders eventually paid up to £600,000 to own one of his originals. His later exhibitions were dedicated to 'The men who laughed at Lowry' and Manchester opened The Lowry Galleries to honour him.

I love that! Don't you just love that? All of us have had, at one time or another, our ideas stamped on, scoffed at or laughed about – and often by those closest to us. All of us have watched the uncouth kick our dream around the floor like a coke can. I love the Lowry story because I have been the butt of many an unkind, 'Who does he think he is?' jibe when I dared to swim against the societal stream. I can take solace in the fact that they laughed at Lowry, and look what happened to him. He became global not only in spite of his detractors, but also perhaps because of them.

I watched a documentary recently about the hugely talented and charismatic (not to mention beautiful) Sheena Easton. It followed her meteoric rise from humble Scottish beginnings to global fame. At one time she had a number one hit record on five different international charts simultaneously. The documentary followed her through her first record deal when her talent was still raw and she was still an unknown. And this is where it was most interesting because she met the lady manager of Lulu (in her prime at the time) who told her, in no uncertain terms, that she did not have the talent or the 'rugged determination' to make it in eighties pop. 'You need a certain something,' she unkindly told the young Easton, 'and you haven't got it.' Oh yeah? The older and more mature Sheena Easton, now a multi-millionaire and one of the most successful British artists of all time would probably disagree.

I can well remember sweeping around the lathe in the middle of a cornflake-sized comfort-zone in middle England, bored to depression. Seeking succour and words of balm I turned to my lathe-turning, jobsworth workmate – elbow-deep in suds, nails full of shit – and half-asked half-stated, 'There's got to be more to life than this.' He laughed, then leaning forward (as though about to tell me a secret) he winked at me – as wise old veterans are inclined to do – 'This is your lot,' he said. 'You should be grateful, this is a job for life.'

It was the 'job for life' bit that scared the tripe out of me. I think he could tell by the slackness of my jaw and the fact that my eyes hit the floor like marbles that his shop-floor philosophy had failed to enlighten. What he said next – not just the words but the bitterness and conviction with which he delivered them – did not. It was like a dry slap across the gob. 'You'll still be here when you're sixty.'

Shortly after my tête-à-tête with Plato of the lathe I snapped my broom (very symbolic) and left the factory forever, never to return. All the things I wanted to do, things I was told I could not, I did. And more. And I am still doing them. This is my life, I can do anything, go anywhere, be whoever I want. We all can. And for those that laugh at my dreams watch out!

You will understand that if you have the intent and the reason you become a watermelon seed with the potential to grow 350,000 times your own size. Can you imagine a small watermelon seed, sat in the shade of a rock, looking admiringly at a huge boulder of a watermelon, and being told by his own mother (watermelon seeds have mums too you know – oh yes they do – humour me, it's an analogy), 'You could be that big if you get from under the shade of this rock.'

I can imagine the baby seed saying, 'You're pulling my plonker mum!' (Though I am not entirely sure that watermelon seeds have plonkers). That's what we are all capable of, and books prove this to us and they encourage and inspire us to do the same. Have you ever read a book that inspired you so much that you wanted to become a rabbit? I did. I kid you not. I read *Watership Down* at a difficult time in my life, I was going through depression as a youth and this book was pivotal in helping (or should I say inspiring) me to move forward. It was one of the most inspiring books I've ever read. In one scene, Hazel, a small and unlikely rabbit, takes on the might of a cat (oh, the bravery); in another scene a rabbit has an epic battle with a dog. A dog! As all the other rabbits run for their dear lives, down holes and over hills, the bravest rabbit in the world (the evil Colonel Woundwort) says, 'What's the matter with you? It's only a dog.' It's only a dog! I love that; don't you love that? When I was depressed I felt like a very small rabbit facing a huge growling dog (my depression). After reading this story, I was inspired into bravery, inspired to fight my own battle against, what appeared on the surface, overwhelming odds.

Books inspire and inspiration is fuel. Where I am now (in the Caribbean) inspires me. Have a good holiday in the Caribbean and I'll defy you not to be inspired.

When I arrived here a week ago, I had no intention of doing anything other than enjoy my holiday, but the beauty of the West Indies inspired me so much that I found myself boundlessly energised. I have been up every morning, sometimes at 4 a.m., to write because the energy is racing around my veins like rabbits down a warren (did we do the rabbit analogy?). It's fantastic, I feel so energised. I wish you could see me now, sat here on deck with a cup of coffee surrounded by the most fantastic life-affirming views, it's like I've died and gone to heaven, it's as though I have fallen into a picture postcard. Inspiration? It's here on tap. When the

Monty Python team wanted to write their classic film *The* of *Brian*, have a guess where they came for inspiration? Here, the Caribbean.

When I was at the Grand Canyon in the Nevada desert I was hugely inspired. The memory of drinking lemonade with Chuck Norris in the Stardust Hotel, Las Vegas, is still inspiring me to this day. Having a coffee with Terry O'Neil (my own hero, a martial arts legend) in the fantastic Lucy in the Sky Café down Cavern Walks (where the Beatles were discovered) in Liverpool inspired the bones off me. Rolling around the judo mat and then talking until 2 a.m. with JKD supremo Rick Young was fuel to my veins. Having dinner with old martial arts legend Peter Consterdine in the Coombe Abbey Hotel, middle England (a luxurious hotel, the best I have ever stayed in), is fixed in my brain like a reserve tank of fuel. I only have to think about it and I get a shot of energy.

I surround myself with successful books, empowering people, awe-inspiring places – how can I not be inspired? I recently had afternoon tea at the Savoy in London (the guest of another inspiring friend, Keith Kernspecht) with Bill, Steve, Keith and his lovely wife and my own wife Sharon. There was so much energy I was overflowing.

A massive shot of inspiration came when I stayed with my lovely friend Martin (a film producer) at his beautiful home in Blackheath, London. We had a great night. When I went to bed at about midnight, Martin gave me two Jim Cartwright scripts that were weeks away from being filmed. I sat up until the early hours reading them. I felt so energised reading twright, in Blackheath after a great night out. It doesn't get any better than that for me.

We are all different, what inspires me might be paint-watchingly dull to you.

I got thirty years of fuel when I watched Bruce Lee doing his thing in the classic film *Enter the Dragon*. It gave me enough fuel (me and millions of others) to get to the higher branches of the martial arts tree. Certainly, I exceeded all expectations, and all thanks to the energy of the late great.

I had a friend who got years of fuel for boxing after watching the film *Rocky*. He only had to listen to the theme tune, 'Eye of the Tiger', and he'd be inspired to hit the gym. Many have been inspired to climb mountains after reading about (or, if they were very fortunate, meeting) Messner, the god of mountaineers.

Motivational tapes give sales people the energy to get out of the car and cold canvass when everything inside them is saying, 'Don't do it,' because they are frightened of rebuttal.

Many people find their fortunes after reading one success book. I had a letter recently from a guy (one of many letters from similar people) who was so inspired by *The Elephant and the Twig* that he packed his bags, tied up a few loose ends and went to New York to play jazz for a living. Another left for Thailand, after reading the same book, to train full-time at a Thai Boxing Camp. One lovely man read *Watch My Back* and took so much inspiration from it that it pulled him from deep depression. He told me later that, but for reading that book, he would have probably killed himself. He was, at the time, manically depressed and no one seemed able to help him. Something in the book gave him hope and he pu ed through. He even went on to work as a doorman himself.

What inspires you? Find out, because what inspires you fires you. If your energy is low or the journey is getting tiresome, pick up that old book and read it again, play the song, watch the film or listen to the cassette that fuels your tanks. Think of it as a long journey, one that needs regular fuel stops. Try not to push yourself so much that you empty the tanks too rapidly, because that means you'll have to continuously stop to re-fuel. The journey is hard, and you don't want to start the same journey twice if you can help it. Once you have broken the inertia, keep the momentum going steadily. It's a lot easier to keep going than it is to keep stop-starting. In other words, don't allow your energy to run out; keep topping it up every few hundred miles and keep searching for new experiences to give you energy, such as new books and tapes, etc. Don't forget that your reasons for wanting success are also a good source of fuel. Recall them, re-run them, and remind yourself why you are there. This will give you extra, much needed fuel.

Only one danger here: there is a time to fuel up and there is a time to get out on the road and motor. It is a delicate balance. No fuel, no journey; too much fuel and you are likely to overflow. You have to get the balance right. Know when to stop putting fuel in the tank. I often make this mistake. I'm all fuelled up, topped to the brim, but fail to recognise (or rather I fail to listen to the signs) that my tank is full. When this happens I tend to end up full to overflowing. I become bloated to the point of either inactivity or displacement. There much energy in me that it overflows into other areas in my life. This can be in the form of irritability, restlessness, sleeplessness, even anger. Don't overfill the tank; once the fuel is in get up and use it, act.

Another problem – which causes a similar frustration – is when people fuel up (they read all the books, listen to all the tapes, attend all the seminars), but fail to cast off. They make a million excuses (of course, if it wasn't for the wife, the mortgage, the kids, life, etc), but the bottom line is they don't move. No point in investing in a ship that isn't ever going to leave port.

Food

Food is a vital source of energy, but there are so many different diets and advice sheets available – each, it seems, contradicting the other – that you never know what is right and what is wrong. And, let's be honest, there is nothing so energy-sapping as those extra folds of weight wrapped around your body like bubble wrap. Go into any bookshop worth its salt and you'll find a pile of books and magazines offering the latest 'lose-fat-and-still-eat-chips' diet that will allow you – money back guaranteed – to have your cake and eat it. Now I don't know about you, but in my time – and as a man with the propensity to grow to the size of a small continent after a two-week holiday in the fat capital, Florida – I have tried them all, and they all work . . . but only for a while.

Almost as soon as you lose the pounds or gain the energy, and the jeans stop creaking at the seams, the very same weight and lack of energy – with a bit extra (for inflation I presume)

– returns with a vengeance and new holes have to be made in your belt to hold the button-bursting balcony creature that has reappeared demanding a large pizza and several beers NOW!

It's so depressing. Isn't it?

It wouldn't be so bad but all the really tasty stuff simply oozes fat. I only have to look at a biscuit barrel and I grow another chin, and as little as a week on a takeaway-fest leaves me with a skin-coloured bumbag that wobbles in time with my step. I can be good for months at a time, sometimes even longer, and my weight stays at a comfortable 13 stone 9, but the minute I get a fry-up down my neck my legs start going all sumo.

When I was 19 and clothes-line thin I could empty the contents of an industrial fridge without clocking up a single number on the bathroom scales. In fact I was so thin I *wanted* to put on weight, but my in-a-hurry metabolism burnt calories as quickly as I could extract them from Kit-Kats and kormas.

Then I hit 30.

At (a very young) 30 I still felt 19, even though my hairline looked a withered 50-something, but my internal calorie-crunching gizmo went on a lazy three-day-week. All of a sudden the nuts and crisps, the beers and curries started to take their toll and I developed what can only be described as a wideload arse, the perfunctory by-product of daring to eat anything more in a day than I burned up. My food-abuse period was over; the salad and chicken renaissance lay in wait.

...om that moment on my weight has gone up and down like a busy lift.

When the weight is off I float around like a light thing in tight fitting T-shirts tucked into bottom hugging jeans, nibbling on health biscuits that taste like manila envelopes. I take every opportunity to remove my top and bare my torso, even when the wind is whipping my nipples into biker studs.

Thin, my esteem and energy rise to the rooftops.

When the weight is on however, a dark cloud descends on my day and my energy levels plummet. My world becomes one of chip dinners (in hide-away greasy spoon cafés), rationalisation, takeaway curries, wine and beer and puddings that I might as well mould right on to my belly. And the apparel changes accordingly too, with beltless trousers, undone at the top two buttons, hidden by trench-coat sweatshirts that hide everything from the neck to the knees. Even sex takes a back seat because it involves nakedness and hours of holding your belly in. Your self-esteem drags around like a wedding trail.

As I said, I have tried them all: high-protein diets that lose you the weight but turn your stools into rocks (ouch); high-fibre diets that have you shitting through the eye of a needle; low-carb diets that leave you so hungry you start nicking food off the kids' plates and snacking on carpet tiles; food-combining diets that are so complicated your brain throbs like a hammered thumb and sends you racing to the nearest chippy for a carb-fat-calorie top up. A man needs his strength after all.

And the fruit diet! What's that all about then? I've attempted it and no matter how hard I tried I cannot make a grape look or taste like a Malteser!

So what is the answer, how do I keep this sylph-like physique with all the culinary temptations constantly battling to fatten me up? How do I keep the weight off and the energy high? As I said earlier, I abstain from foods that make me feel sluggish. I try to avoid the rubbish whenever I can but after 40 years of counting calories, hunting for the fat content on the backs of crisp packets and watching my bungee-belly bounce back and forward from six pack to beer barrel, I've come to the conclusion that disciplined light eating, for the rest of my stay on this spinning blue thing in the cosmos, is the only way to stop me from looking like a doughnut. It's hard, and you can never let up but it works. Have some of what you want, but not all of what you want, train every other day and you'll keep the fat-monster at bay.

I live in hope that the hereafter might be a paradoxical universe where Mars bars and crisp sandwiches are the vital sustenance of life. In the meantime I'm going to heed my mum's advice – offered to me when I hit a hefty 16 stone and had to take out a second postcode on my arse – 'Walk *past* that chip shop Geoffrey.'

So act, fuel up and . . . go!

But when you do go make sure that you keep your balance. How do you do that? Let me tell you first thing in the morning.

- Secret Eight -

The Power of Balance

5 a.m. West Indies – 11 January 2001

It's a gorgeous morning. The sun is not up yet and a large portion of the Caribbean Sea is still lit up by the moon. I'm feeling rested and happy as the ship cruises towards the island of St Kits.

I promised last night that I would talk about balance. So many people seem to be out of it – I have been myself, many times – so I thought I'd better enter it into the book as secret number eight. I mean, it's not as though you can to go the chemist and pick up a prescription for 'balance' with your cough medicine and your condoms. Putting it bluntly, balance, when you are out of plumb, can, does, did and will make you poorly.

I have to tell you that I have spent a lot of time out of balance. I was the 'out of balance' master; I could do lectures on the stuff. I've actually been ill many times due to this unspoken-about phenomenon. Is balance a part of success? Yes, oh yes, it is an imperative part. Can you be successful without it? Well that really depends upon your definition of success. I've been at the top of many trees and (to the outside world) a success, but I've been ill, negligent to those I love and unhappy. So I didn't consider myself a success. When you barter health for wealth, and family for fortune, you come out a sorry second place. I don't think it's a good investment when you bet a pound to win a penny.

I know that we have the capabilities to bring all our dreams to manifestation. All of them. The world is at our fingertips and it is very exciting. But reaching your goal should not be at the cost of everything good in your life.

Now there is a paradox at play here. I am fond of saying that to have your dreams you have to be prepared to risk all, and I believe that. But the risk (on the surface a very large one) is calculated. As in: I am prepared to risk all. I will handle the worst-case scenario, but I will also employ every measure I can to make sure that worst-case scenario never happens. For instance, if your spouse is against your plans to succeed you have to ask yourself: is she right to be against me? Does she have a point? Can I learn from her objections? And ultimately: am I prepared to go on regardless and risk the love of this woman?

I had this problem with my first wife. A lovely girl, but not a lady who wanted to take on the unpredictability of a road less travelled. She was (and still is) a 'beaten track' kind of lass, and that's OK for her but not for me. When she pointed out holes in my plan I had to ask myself, 'Is she right, are there flaws in my thinking, should I be grateful just to have a regular nine-to-five like she said or is she just scared?' After careful consideration and many talks (with me asking her to please support me, and her telling me to be happy with what I'd got) I decided that it was the latter. Then came the ultimate question, 'Am I prepared to lose this lady for my dreams?' I guess I was, because she is now my ex-wife. That sounds harsh I know, and to be honest I don't ever remember making such a cold decision. All I know is that I left my comfort-zone on my own and when I grew I outgrew my lady. I became a very different person to the one that she wanted in her life; I became the person *I* wanted to be. She didn't like the new me, so love went belly-up and in time – a very painful time – I moved on. Sad, but as Esther might say, 'That's life.'

I am often asked this question by potential conquistadors, 'My wife/husband will not support me, what should I do?' First you have to ask yourself whether you are prepared to risk all, and be brutally honest with your answer. If the answer is 'no', then there is nothing more I can offer, other than to hazard a guess that the relationship probably won't last anyway. Resentment is born the moment those we love say that they will not support our dreams; and that resentment will grow in the void where your entrepreneurial spirit once resided. Love is about giving two seemingly paradoxical things, roots and wings. The moment you kill the wings by placing a cage around your love is the very first moment you allow love to become control. I know, in my past I have been a wing-clipper myself, to the detriment of the relationship. So lay the question on the table and if your answer is, 'No, I will not risk all,' then get back on with your life and do your best to live with your decision (remember here, we are talking about a situation where your partner is not prepared to support your aspirations. If you have the right person you can make your goal together with no risk to the relationship. The question only arises when you are forced to choose). Don't allow yourself to blame your spouse. You made the decision after all. If your answer were 'yes', I'd say your next step is to move mountains to try and encourage him/her to take the journey with you. People do not want to grow because they are scared of leaving comfort-zones. Try to alleviate their fear, communicate with them, let them see how passionate you are about your aims, tell them how much they are loved, how precious they are to you and how you want, with all your heart, to share your vision with them. Communicate. That means an honest heart-to-heart, not dictation, not threats and not bullying. 'Please support me, I love you and need your help.'

It didn't work for me; my lady knew what she wanted – I can't blame her for that – and made it very clear that she had made her choice and that I should make mine.

I have never regretted my ultimate decision. Where I am is where I wanted to be. In retrospect the pain of separation and ultimately divorce were a large part of what I needed to forget my mentality. You might think me selfish, and I guess I am, but it's what Charles Handy would call 'proper selfishness'. It was good for me, but it's also been good for everyone else concerned. My ex-wife wanted me to be someone I couldn't be. If I had complied our life would have been a façade, a lie. That is not the kind of heritage I want to pass on to my kids.

Communicate. Communication is all.

So success is getting to the winning line in one piece. Not making yourself ill in the process. It is about keeping one eye firmly on the goal and another on your health and your relationships. You can work as hard as you like (and you will have to work very hard) but you also need an equal amount of play and rest. Life, don't forget, is about being happy and if you are working it's easy to forget to rest and have fun. I admire work ethic. It is (as I have said) an imperative, but please, make time to rest and play also. That's where the balance lies. Work, rest and play in equal proportions.

Recently (you may or may not be aware) I just completed a 32-city book-signing tour. Very arduous, we probably visited somewhere in the region of 50 to 60 shops in a 6-week period. When I started the tour, the very thought overwhelmed me, but I knew that if I kept balanced I would not only make it, I'd make it in good style; and so I did. But only because I turned the trip into a balanced adventure, where we travelled by train (so we could read and relax) stayed in nice hotels and treated each city like we were going there on holiday. We stayed in lovely rooms, ate well, meditated whenever the opportunity allowed, did some sightseeing and delegated the work back home to my gorgeous daughter Lisa so that we didn't have to come back to massive workloads. Before we started the tour we had a week at Centre Parks (a fabulous holiday resort set in thousands of acres of Sherwood Forest) and when we finished we planned to take this Caribbean Cruise so that we could recuperate. I felt as good at the end of the tour as I did at the beginning, because I managed to balance all the way through. I believe that any goal can be achieved (and be the better for it) with balance. Work hard, rest hard, and play hard.

There is a tendency, once you get stuck into work, rest or play, to get out of balance. People who play too hard get no work done and don't rest. People who rest too much tend to get no work and no play, they become lazy. And as I said, those who work too much often do so to the detriment of all else. Don't do it! Work hard, yes, but rest and play because balance is healthy, balance is happy.

There is a grey area however. When you love what you do, as I do, the work stops being work, it becomes play too, even rest because it relaxes me. If this is the case – I truly hope it is – then you are often getting all three in one. If your family work with you, as Sharon does with me, even better, but be aware, your balance may be out of sync with theirs. On our last tour, I was so busy getting my own balance right, that I didn't notice Sharon getting out of balance. Consequently, she got ill on the tour and it was a very worrying time. Also, because I love what I do there is often the danger of becoming a bore (me? no never). People come to visit and all I talk about is business (to them it is business: to me it is great fun). Often my eldest girls come to see me and I find my time taken up with phone calls or conversations based around the business. So take time, make time for those who perhaps do not want to talk about the premise of your next project or how exciting your life is. Listen to the energy around you, and heed it. There is a time for you, for your things, but make sure there is also a time for others and for their things. Let others have their moment. I am still working on this myself.

Listen to Your Body

As I said earlier in the book, your body hears everything you say, but it also talks to you (it says things like, 'Get me a chocolate bar and a curry!'). It gives you messages to let you know how it is coping. Listen and heed or suffer the consequences. When it gives you rest signs, rest. I go into greater detail in *A Book for the Seriously Stressed* but some of the signs I have noticed are:

Irritability
Impatience
Intolerance of others
Anger
Paranoia
The urge to over-eat
The urge to use the toilet more
Sleeplessness
Irrational thought
Quick to temper
Crying easily
Restlessness

To be honest, anything out of the ordinary is a sign that something is up. Take a break. You may only need an hour or a day, but it could be a week or two. Pop stars, prolific workers, are often forced to take long breaks because overwork makes them ill. Believe me when you are in the land of bad health you'll gladly swap all the wealth for even a day of respite. But you can stop it before it starts by balancing your life. It is no coincidence that so many pop stars these days are getting into yoga and Tai Chi. Both of these pastimes are fabulous for bringing balance to a body and mind in turmoil. Check one or the other out and make it a part of your life. Above all listen to your body. When it gives you pain and discomfort it is trying to tell you something. Listen. Your body knows best.

Also get some physical training into your life; it clears the rubbish, the toxins from your body. Be balanced with your food, have some of what you want but not all of what you want and none of what harms you, like drugs. All work and no play make Johnny a dull boy. Work, rest and play. Keep your eye on the goal, listen to the energy, it tells you all you need to know, but it doesn't help if you don't heed.

There's one more thing. Along the path take time out to help others. There is a secret benefit to benevolence. I'll tell you why in the next chapter.

– Secret Nine –

The Power of Tithing

6 a.m. 12 January 2001

Tithing is an ancient philosophy, yet it still remains largely unknown. So it is secret number nine in the art of loving your life and living your dreams.

To be honest, this wonderful vehicle to greater prosperity even remains a secret to many people who know it, they've heard of it, but they either don't believe or understand it. I'm not 100 per cent sure that I fully understand it myself to be honest, I don't understand the theory of electricity either, but that doesn't stop me from turning the light on every morning when I'm looking for clean socks. Understand it I do not, believe it and employ it I certainly do. All the time, and to great effect.

Tithing is the art (and it is an art that needs to be developed) of giving, the art of charity. The Bible is full to the brim with examples of tithing, of giving to receive, of benevolence being a reciprocal experience. Most of the holy books talk of giving one tenth of your gross income to good deeds and when you do, your tithe is returned tenfold. Most of these books were written a very long time ago and interpretations are many and varied, often contradictory. What we can be sure of is the fact that giving to others is a good thing, even if there is absolutely no return. Helping others and becoming very good at it, needs to be an imperative in a world that is in danger of becoming 'I'm-alright-Jack' selfish. I can't start this chapter without admitting that I don't, yet, give enough. But I am working very hard on it. There is a lot of fear in giving and paradoxically it is fear that blocks the way to more prosperity. It takes courage, faith and discipline to believe that, by giving, you won't end up down Stony Broke Street. So I've been spending the past umpteen years perfecting the art of giving. I have never given yet when it has not been returned in full, and with profit. The more I have given the more I have received. It is as though in giving I have created a vacuum, and as we should all know nature abhors a vacuum and will redress the balance when one is created. The Bible talks about giving ten per cent as a minimum, but it talks in monetary terms. I know from experience that, in reality, whatever you give comes back to you. Cast your bread out on to the water and it will return tenfold. So the more you give the more you get back.

REMEMBER – the rewards of giving may not always come back from the person to whom you first gave..

Tithing is fantastically available to us all. There is always something to give; it doesn't have to be money. You may think you do not have enough to tithe. You do, we all do.

We all have something to give; even if it is just your time. Time is currency you know. We all have at least that to give. I have read a lot of books about (or by) fabulously wealthy men and women. I have not read one yet who did not tithe. Most do not say it outright because (I believe) they are observing the modesty law that says the only real charity is anonymous. I happen to agree with this law. I recommend to people that their good deeds be from the heart and not from the PR sheet. It can also be a smile, a wave, a healing or forgiving thought, a letter to a friend or a sympathetic ear, it can be one pound to a down-and-out, a genuine handshake, you can give love, hope, faith, a flower from your back garden, you can give understanding. There is room for everyone, and everyone has room if they will only step into their own promised land. When the Hebrews found the Promised Land it took them forty years to move into it. They were in the wilderness yet when they spied their land of milk and honey they refused to enter. Why? After a lifetime of incarceration and wandering, they could not actually believe what they'd found. Hence they sat on the periphery of paradise talking about their fears of walled cities and wild beasts, about enemies and dangers. They feared that entering would lead to death. The opposite was true of course. In fact the ones who feared death found it in the wilderness. Once the doubters had perished the entire Hebrew nation entered their promised land in three days. It happened very quickly once they accepted the truth.

Tithing is a fast-track way to your own promised land, but you have to strip away the walls of fear before you can savour the milk and honey. You have to have the courage to exit the wilderness before you can enter. So, if you are a little apprehensive, try it first, give a little and see if I'm not right. Then as your confidence grows give more and more. In fact give as much as you want to receive. The bigger your tithe, the more you give, the more you get back. It is 'proper selfishness'. When you give to others you are actually giving to yourself. So why not give more? Fear? I know how you feel. But the boundaries of your fear can be stretched until eventually there are no limits to your philanthropy. The very act of not giving hints at fear and fear blocks the way to greater prosperity, so if you want more, give more.

The Bible actually recommends that you deliberately tithe if there is something you specifically want. They suggest that the reason your want is not forthcoming is because you have not created space for it by giving. So give to make the space for what you want.

In this age, most of us already give when we pay our taxes. Our taxes pay for our National Health Service, road maintenance, schools, etc. but it also helps those who cannot or will not work, for whatever reason. So in paying tax we all tithe, but many of us do it grudgingly. I know I used to hate looking at my pay packet with 30 per cent missing, I begrudged paying tax but I was ignorant. I didn't realise that tax was a great way to give a proportion of my income to help those worse off than me. Now I put money in a separate account every week in anticipation of my tax bill. I don't even see that money as mine and I give it gladly. I know now that it's a tithe and that it will come back to me. All of it and more.

My life is full of great examples of the power of tithing, every day I give and receive, sometimes in the simplest ways. I am not trying to make converts of everyone here, only to say that this is a fast-track method of getting what you want from others, by giving others what they want. If you want happiness, give it to others; if you want success or money help someone else to get success and money. Whatever you want take time to help others and it will be returned in kind. There is room for everyone, and everyone has room.

As most of you may or may not know I have been involved in the martial arts for many years, about thirty now. In my time I have seen many great examples of successful tithing. I have watched people go from guarded and cynical existences (because they could not, would not, or did not give) to living happy, healthy and hugely prosperous lives because they learnt to give. When you talk to these fellows they can't wait to give you their secrets to wealth and prosperity, they can't wait to give you a piece of their cake. And why? Because they have discovered the art of tithing. The ones who have nothing? Well, they're easy to spot because they are in receipt of what they have given – usually hatred, suspicion, cynicism and distrust.

Tithing works for good and for bad (it is a karmic thing). You tithe fear, distrust and hate and you will draw it to you in abundance. If you tithe the suspicion and deceit, have a guess what you'll get back – that's right, suspicion and deceit, in abundance. As I said, this life of ours is a reciprocal experience, you get what you give. Like a boomerang our thoughts, words and deeds are returned to us in kind. This is not the work of a vengeful God; rather it is a work of our own making. Your life is a self-portrait and you're the guy with the oils and the canvas. What would you draw for yourself? Because what you put on the canvas is on show for all to see. So if your life is not the oil painting you hoped it would be don't look outside of yourself for someone to blame. You are the guy that puts the colours on your portrait, no one else. If they don't fit your ideal then change them, but remember: what you give becomes you, literally. If you want more kindness in your life then start being kind to others. If you want people to get back to you on the phone, try getting back to those who are of no obvious profit to you. You want love, respect, and compassion? Give it in abundance and you'll be shouting at the top of your voice, 'Enough love/respect/compassion already, I've got too much as it is!' What do you want? Anything! Give it to others. Spend even just your spare time giving and you'll have a full-time job reaping the returns. When those returns start arriving at your door (with the postman complaining about the weight of his postbag) give a proportion away. Never complain when people write to you for help, advice, solace, guidance, never allow yourself a moment's complaint when your door knocker is falling off from over-use, because every call you get, every knock, is God sending you work, and work with the best pay day you'll ever get. If you want wealth in your life, in whatever form, then start by giving wealth to others, or helping others to get wealth. Sir Winston Churchill once said that many people stumble upon the truth, but they get back up and walk away as though nothing happened. Because the truth, the secret, is *too* simple. People are so busy looking for some complex alchemistic formula to make gold that they fail to see the riches right in front of their eyes. Tithing is the best way I know of getting what you want from life by giving to others. Do you get it? There are diamonds in the back garden of every man, woman and child. You've just got to recognise them for what they are and then have the discipline to go diamond-picking. People say to me, 'Thank you for helping me.' No! Thank *you*, why would I turn you away when God sent you?

Give and it will be given unto thee.

Try it, what have you got to lose?

When should you try?

Well, now of course, because *now* is the only real time we have. That's secret number ten.

The Power of Now

6.30 a.m. 13 January 2001

Now, of course, is the time to act, either to achieve your goal or (at the very least) step on to the first rung of the ladder. Leaders throughout history have all realised the same truth, that now is the only time we have so now is exactly when we should act. I carry a notebook with me everywhere I go, and I mean everywhere, because great ideas are always coming to me and if I don't note them down immediately, I tend to lose them. I'll get home and think, 'What was that flash of inspiration, that great idea I had earlier?' And you know what, I can never remember, it's gone. How many great intuitive flashes of brilliance have you let go? In fact how many ideas have you failed to act upon, for whatever reason, that have later proved to be winners when used by someone who didn't hesitate?

I remember one occasion when I had a flash of brilliance, a great idea that sparked in my mind, in the middle of a book-signing tour. The idea was to mail drop all my mail-order customers, about 7,000 at the time, and offer them a special deal. My customers had been great; very loyal and supportive. Why not, I asked myself, reward those on my mailing list by offering them a buy-two-get-one-free deal that could give them as much as a £25 item for free if they bought two other products (tithing)? Not the most original idea in the world, but new for me. The problem was, mailing 7,000 people means a lot of work, and because I was in the middle of a book-signing tour, time was at a premium. I made time. The perfect time to try my idea out was there and then. I felt that if I didn't act immediately, the moment would be lost. I didn't have the time, that's true, but I had a great family who did. I asked my wife and children to muck in. They agreed without hesitation and within a week, we'd mailed 7,000 people with the special offer. Seeing as I was visiting stores and shops all around the country promoting my new book, I thought it might also be a good idea to place a little leaflet in every one of the 7,000 letters saying, 'By the way, I am in these cities signing books and giving free lectures. If you'd like to pop in, I'd love to see you.' It was the most successful mail drop I've ever done. We doubled the gross of a normal mail drop. Of those who bought a book or video, 80 per cent went for the quid pro quo deal. Also we had record numbers supporting the book tour. Which was a bonus we could not have realised if I'd not acted immediately. We think there is time ahead of us, but the only real time to write the letter, make the phone call, present the proposal, offer the apology is now, in the present moment.

In my youth, I had massive ambitions to write for TV; plays, sketches, I even had film ideas. But they never really went beyond the idea stage. Oh, I wrote some of them down, showed them to friends, but I never sent them off, or if I did I only did it once, and failed to follow up. Do you know how many of those ideas I've had to sit and watch appear on my TV screen over the years. My ideas, written and sent in by others who'd had the same notion but unlike me, they acted upon it? I'm frightened and embarrassed to tell you, but it is a very large amount. Now I write everything down. I send everything off. I have stage plays, cinema films, books, stationery ideas, T-shirt deals (and more) all out there working for me at this moment in time. I eat now by harvesting the crop from last year's seeds, I'll eat next year from the crop of the seeds I plant today. My entrepreneurial seeds are well and truly planted. And if the seeds are planted in fertile ground they will bear fruit. If I get an idea, I do something with it. Lots of people say to me, 'I've got this great idea,' and they tell me their premise and, more often than not I think, wow, that really is a great idea. But very few ever get beyond the drawing board stage because the intention to manifest that idea is not there, only the dream is present and a dream is not real until you mix in the magic ingredient – intent. Do it now, this very moment. Some people stay up all night talking about it, others stay up all night doing it.

I was at a local petrol station in Coventry paying for my diesel when a young chap approached me, hand extended, 'Mr Thompson, I'd like to shake your hand.' I didn't know this chap from Adam, but I shook his hand, whilst at the same time asking, 'So why do you want to shake my hand?' He went on to tell me how he'd heard me on the radio talking about my book *The Elephant and the Twig* and my premise that by acting in the now we could change our lives for the better. 'I was working in the factory,' he continued, 'but I hated every minute and every hour. Then I heard you on the radio, a guy that's worked in a factory just like me, saying that if we didn't like our lot we could change it, right away if we wanted to.' He must have really wanted to because he did no more than walk right into the foreman's office, that moment, and hand in his resignation. 'Now I run my own business,' he said, 'that's my van out there.' He pointed out on to the forecourt and right enough there it was, a van with his name and logo printed on the side. He acted in the now, while his inspiration was hot and before others (and himself) talked him out of it. He didn't like his job, this much he already knew, but his job didn't own him and he had the power to change it the moment this truth became his reality.

I spent 7 years in a factory job working continental shifts. Mornings that started very early, afternoons that seemed to eat up the whole day and night shifts that left you indescribably tired and unable to do much of anything. Whilst on nights (for me this shift was hell itself) it was as though my whole life stopped. I dreaded them so much that even now, 20 years later, I still have nightmares about being back there. I only have to talk to someone who is working nights and it is as though I'm there again. I stuck it out for 7 years. Why? Because back then I felt as though I had no other choice and every time I courted the idea that there were greener pastures,

someone (my wife, friends or workmates) conv;
otherwise. I say convinced, they scared the pants off
offering reminders of how bad it was 'out there' and how
my mortgage and my life were connected to my present
employ. They scared me off. I scared myself off by listening
to them and allowing them to kill my inspiration. In the end
they didn't even need to speak, I told myself. I knew the
script, after all, I'd heard it enough times. Ironically, most of
the people I was allowing to determine my life's path are
people I can't even put a name to now. Have a look around
at some of your detractors and ask yourself, 'Will I even know
these people in ten years' time?' Then one day I stopped
listening to them, I was tired of hating my life. I was in a
prison and do you know who was keeping me there, do you
know who had the key? Me! I was the keeper of the key, I
was the jailer, and I was the jail. It wasn't the others; they
couldn't hold me back — not even if they tried all at once —
not if I didn't want them to. I was (and I am) a member of the
most powerful and creative species on this spinning planet. I
was (and I am) a lion amongst the sheep and there was (and
there is) not a single mortal thing that could cage me if I really
want to escape. I stopped blaming the world for my very
sorry lot. I kicked myself up the backside and did what I should
have done years before. I left the job I hated and started to
live (and live I did). I prospered. Was I scared? You bet I was.
But my intention to be better than I had been up until then
became so hot that it burned the fear I felt as fuel. The fear
helped me reach heights I'd only ever dreamed of. So many
people said, 'You're a fool, it's a mistake, you'll be back.' I

didn't let them stop me and later I came to realise that liberation is always attacked by those still imprisoned in dull lives, they envy your courage to grow, to leave your comfort-zone (and theirs, don't forget we share our comfort-zones with others). Secondly, I realised that whilst you must always stand your corner and fight for your right to liberation and change, you must also try to find compassion and understanding for those left behind even, and perhaps especially, if they condemn and attack you.

Excuses

Tomorrow; maybe the next day; soon; after the weekend; one of these days; when the time is right; when the circumstances are better; when I've got the money; when I know a bit more. Have you ever used any of these excuses? I've used them all at one time or another, sometimes all at once. Always putting off the first move, not having the guts to take the initiating step that will break the inertia and get me going. None of the above times are ever the right time to start, I can tell you this without even knowing who you are, or without knowing your goal and really you know it anyway, I'm just reminding you. The only real time we have is now. All the other times don't exist. Yesterday is a picture postcard of a time that died. Tomorrow is a mind's-eye promise that may never come. For some, tomorrow has already gone. We think we can barter with our tomorrows and that there will be time, the 'right time' as we tell ourselves; we cannot and there is not. There is a poignant Japanese proverb that says, 'Young man seize every moment of your time, the days fly by, ere long you too shall grow old, you too shall die. If you believe me not see here in the courtyard how the frost glistens white and cold and cruel on the grass that once was green.'

Make the phone call now, take the decision now, break the inertia right this moment. Place the deposit for the dream holiday (or even just go), make the stretch for the dream car, the dream house, the dream girl or boy. Now, now, now.

Phew. I'm off for a decaff.

Blame

One of the things that stop us from making the move, breaking the inertia is blame. We blame others for our lot. I talk a lot about blame in my books because blame is what I allowed to keep me rooted for so very long. I fell – like so many – into the blame trap. Our influences – as I said earlier – are so important. But ultimately we that choose our influences. We often feel that if we could change outside influence – or if they would change to accommodate us – all would be well. Yeah right! If fish would jump out of the sea into baskets it'd save the fisherman having to go out on boats and catch them. If our employers would just send us a bit of cash in a brown envelope once a week it'd save us having to go out to work. It's the big IF. If my Auntie Jane had a beard and whiskers (come to think of it she does) she'd be my Uncle John. The world will not change to accommodate us, but it doesn't have to, if we only change ourselves. If you change your perception of the world, you change your world. If you change your perception, you change everything. Two men look through prison bars, one sees mud the other stars. Blake, the great poet, said that the mind was a place of its own and that we could make it a heaven or we could make it a hell.

I read recently about a guy that was sent to prison for life. His crime is not important in this story, how he handled his jail term is. He had choices, he could have blamed circumstances for his lot, he could have rebelled against the system, and he could have laid back and wasted his life away. Many have and many more will. He could, like many, have thought, 'Well, that's my life over,' and in prison, if you have the wrong perception or a negative mental attitude it most certainly is. He managed – just by changing his frame of mind – to turn his prison into a haven, a cell into a university, a life of hell into an idealist heaven. This particular man accepted responsibility for his lot. He didn't blame anyone, he didn't rebel. What he did do was indulge his life long passion for architecture. He loved buildings, he had a passion for them, so he did something that he'd always wanted to do, he studied them full-time. And one thing is for sure; he did have plenty of time. He studied night and day. Before long this positive and empowering inmate became an expert in architecture. His reputation grew, even from his prison cell, and people from the outside world started to write to him for advice or information on certain buildings and structures. His knowledge grew and before long he got a reputation as a world-renowned authority, eventually the world authority on architecture. Can you imagine that? That's so inspiring. The world's number one expert, the authority on architecture and all from a prison cell.

Whenever I fall into the blame trap or think the world is not being kind to my needs, I think about this fellow and it kicks me up the backside, it re-energises me. If he can do it from a prison cell, with all those restrictions (lack of liberty being the main one) what could I do with an open world? Looking at it like that, there's nothing I can't do. Don't try and change the world, change the man. And do it now.

There's a lovely story about a Reverend in his study trying to come up with a talk-topic for the Sunday service. He was struggling a little, not least because his five-year-old son was hovering around him, patently bored. To give the boy something to do, the Reverend took out an old magazine and flipped through the pages until he came to a map of the world. He tore the page out of the magazine and then proceeded to tear the map page into small pieces – like bits of a jigsaw. He then threw the pieces all around the front room floor. 'When you can place all the pieces together,' he told his son, 'and make the map of the world, bring it to me and I'll give you a dollar.' The Reverend went back to his work, sure in the belief that the task would take his son most of the morning. After ten minutes or so the boy returned to the study with the completed map of the world. The Reverend was amazed. 'How did you manage to do it so quickly?' He asked incredulously.

'Oh, it was easy,' the boy replied. 'On the back of the page with the map on was a picture of a man. Once I got the man right, the world got right all by itself.'

And so the Reverend got a great topic for his Sunday Mass: Get the man right and the world will get right all by itself.

Oh, and do it now, because it's the only time we have.

– Epilogue –

A Word of Warning

It's New Year, a great time for new beginnings, and a fabulous period for casting aside the old to make room for the new. The air is high with excitement and expectation and a multitude of fresh ideas and business ventures flourish with the new calendar. But be careful whom you talk to as you plant those seedlings, because inspiration can quickly turn to desperation if you plant in the wrong soil (in other words be careful who you share your dreams with). It could all end in tears before it has even begun.

Liam was very excited about the prospect of starting the New Year on a positive note. His resolution was to work for himself and give up the nine-to-five torture that had become his prison. He wanted my opinion; did I think he could do it?

By the time we had finished talking – I was with him for an hour and three coffees – the energy was hot; he was going to change the world with his innovative ideas and concepts. He couldn't wait to get started. I was excited for him. He was/is a hugely charismatic man who had already achieved some impressive personal goals in his life. Starting a business in a field where he excelled seemed the natural way forward. After all, self-employment was the only goal (thus far) that had eluded him, and he dreamed of being his own boss. When I left Liam, still high on the conversational plans, he was all set to change his world. It was obvious to me (and everyone that knew him) that this man could move mountains if he set his mind to it. You can imagine my surprise when, one week later, he rang me with the news that he had kicked his plans into touch. His week-old enthusiasm had disappeared only to be replaced by a cynicism that stole the energy right out of the air. He started the telephone conversation by telling me that he'd had second thoughts about his business venture and concluded by insisting that, 'No business is worth sacrificing the youth of your children and the love of your wife for.'

Excuse me? Did I miss something here?

I was talking to a complete stranger. The infant entrepreneur had vanished down my phone line. And he was angry too. At me! I'd encouraged his ideas and by inference suggested his business was more important than his family. I had a fair idea what had happened.

'Who've you been talking to Liam?' I asked after suffering minutes of defensive procrastination (his, not mine).

'Well,' he said, sheepishly, 'I talked to a couple of guys at the gym and they told me the crack!'

'The crack?' I enquired.

'The crack! About working for yourself? When they were in business they were doing 80 hours a week and never got to see their kids and one of them ended up in the divorce courts and…'

I think you get the picture.

What was a great idea, a revolutionary concept, a world-changing inspiration had suddenly, over the space of seven days and a couple of negative conversations, become the worst idea since the Incontinence Thong. His positive thoughts had been swamped by the negative words of others. Their thoughts had become his.

Now don't get me wrong here, I'm not suggesting for even a second that Liam (or you) should not do a little market research into your idea or dream; in fact I would insist that h___d. Neither am I saying that the pros and cons of any new venture should not be fully explored, I would expect no less. But if you want to go into business in a successful way don't just talk to people with an MA in Business Failure because all you're going to get is a thesis on woe and doom.

Neither is it wise to seek advice from the uninitiated or from those invested in seeing you fail and there are plenty of those about I have to tell you. If you want to be a champion swimmer, better to speak to the ripply-thing doing fast lengths in the deep end than the chap stood in the shallows with a (skin-coloured) rubber ring and a float. The latter can teach you a lot about how to sink – and there can be lessons in that – but hang around for too long and you might end up on the bottom of the pool yourself.

Take advice, it's important, take constructive criticism, it'll help you to grow, but remember this: the moment a new idea or concept is formed in your mind is a pivotal one. When the lobster sheds his shell he is free to grow but at the same time he is also vulnerable to prey because he is without protection. It is often at this point that negatives tend to fly in; if you are not careful you might find yourself, like Liam, aborting the flight before your wheels have even left the runway.

Your ideas and aspirations are important and should not be shared with doubting Thomas's (even if they are family members). By injecting doubt in your mind – even inadvertently – when your ideas are first taking seed, they can cause distress and an abortion of even the best-laid plans.

A great idea that has been laced with fear and doubt is a three-legged donkey in a world of thoroughbreds so please, take my advice, if you want to be a millionaire (as they say) hang around millionaires.

The sun is rising over Barbados, the decaff is hot at my lips and breakfast is cooking on deck behind me.

I am at one of the most beautiful locations in the world, my beautiful wife on my arm and I have to tell you, it really does not get any better than this.It wasn't always this way. As the skyline meets the sea and the lights of Barbados come into view I reflect on days gone by when discontentment and perplexity were my travel companions. Discontentment because I felt life should be more than lathe-turning and factory fortnights in holiday camps that did little to inspire. Perplexity because I couldn't understand why things were not better. I am not talking regret here. My first marriage did not work, but the four children that it bore are beautiful beyond my ability to describe in written words.

No regrets. When you love your babies more than life itself (and when they love you back just as hard) the word regret does not even come into it. Anyway, what's there to regret? I've got a kicking life, I love it. When I look in the mirror I like the man that looks back. Even more so because he is a walking manifestation of every experience – good and bad – that I ever had. To change even one element of my journey thus far would be to change who I am and what I have become. I don't want to do that. What I do want is to pass on my life lessons (to my babies and to you) so that you might realise early that life is for living right now, and that although we often feel tied we never really are. We can break the twig and make the Great Escape any time we want.

As the Caribbean Sea splashes over the deck and on to the pages of this book, and the ocean lights blue with a new morning, I sit and contemplate the beauty of life, the joy of another day and I thank God for every moment of it.

Thank you for reading *The Great Escape*, I hope you enjoyed it. It's time for me to close the pad now, my breakfast is ready and it's time for me to climb my next mountain. So, from one elephant to another, weighing more than any imposed or supposed limitation, I say this: Yank that twig out of the ground, mud, roots and all, and make today the first day of your new life, an exciting incarnation, where you love your life and live your dreams.

May your God bless you as mine has me.

Geoff Thompson
(aboard the Sunbird cruise ship, sipping coffee, somewhere in the Caribbean Sea).

COULD YOU BE A BODYGUARD?

YES. WITH THE RIGHT TRAINING YOU PROBABLY COULD

We need men & women to train as "Close Protection Officers"
This could be the new and exciting career that you deserve.
Apply now for a free information pack.
You've nothing to lose
(Except maybe that dreary 9 to 5 existence)
Call 01372 726252
or write to: Excel Protection. The Coach House, West St, Epsom, KT18 7RL

NATURE'S ⟨tree⟩ BEST

Unit 13/15 • Victoria Way • Studlands Park • Newmarket • CB8 7SH
Tel: 01638 662589   Fax: 01638 665922

Nature's Best, suppliers of high quality nutritional and dietary support products, supply and sponsor Geoff Thompson with all his nutritional and dietary support requirements.

We wish Geoff every possible success for the future and thank him for the mental stimulation supplied by his books!

Mike Wilson,
Managing Director,
Nature's Best